D1634747

Your Guide to Irish Law

Mary Faulkner
Gerry Kelly
Padraig Turley

GILL & MACMILLAN

Published in Ireland by
Gill & Macmillan Ltd
Goldenbridge
Dublin 8
with associated companies throughout the world
© Mary Faulkner, Gerry Kelly, Padraig Turley 1993
0 7171 1964 5
Index compiled by Helen Litton
Print origination by O'K Graphic Design, Dublin
Printed by
ColourBooks Ltd, Dublin

All rights reserved. No part of this publication may be copied,
reproduced or transmitted in any form or by any means, without
permission of the publishers.

A catalogue record is available for this book
from the British Library.

1 3 5 4 2

CONTENTS

ABORTION

An abortion was regarded in Irish law, from 1861 until recently, as an unlawful termination of pregnancy. It was an offence for a woman, or any other person, to cause or attempt to cause an abortion. The Offences Against the Person Act, 1861 provided that if the woman herself was charged it was essential that she was pregnant at the time of the attempt, whereas in the case of any other person it was immaterial whether the woman was pregnant or not. The penalty was penal servitude for life.

Abortion was not regarded in law as murder because the unborn had no existence independent of the mother. The law of homicide applies only where the victim has been born.

Supplying poisons, instruments, etc., knowing that they were to be used to cause an abortion, was also a crime and carried the penalty of five years' penal servitude.

The sale, importation, manufacture, advertising or display of abortifacients was prohibited under the 1979 Family Planning Act.

In 1983 the Eighth Amendment to the Constitution was enacted acknowledging the right to life of the unborn with due regard to the equal right to life of the mother. Which right prevailed when the two were in conflict remained undecided until the Supreme Court decision of March 1992 in the X case. It was held by the court in that case that abortion was lawful where there was a real and substantial risk to the life of the mother, including a risk from self-destruction, risks which could only be avoided by the termination of the pregnancy. It was also held that an injunction could be granted to prevent a woman travelling out of this state for the purpose of obtaining an abortion where that abortion would not be lawful here. This decision proved controversial and the issue remained open with legislation and a referendum promised.

On 25 November 1992 the people of Ireland were asked to decide the matter in three referenda. These referenda concerned:

(1) The right to information on abortion services abroad
(2) The right to travel to obtain an abortion
(3) The right to abortion in this state where the life of the mother (as opposed to the health) is at risk.

Two of the three referenda were carried and so the constitution has been amended. On the right to information issue there is now the freedom to obtain or make available, in this state, information on abortion services lawfully available in another state. This is however subject to such conditions as may be laid down by law i.e. legislation.

On the right to travel issue there is now the freedom to travel between this state and another state. This provides that any woman may travel abroad for an abortion for any reason.

On the 'substantive issue' (the abortion issue) the proposal was to limit the Supreme Court decision in the X case by specifying that the risk must be to the life, as distinct from the health, of the mother and by excluding the risk of self-destruction from the category of risks which might allow abortion. As this proposal was not carried, the Supreme Court decision in the X case stands and the legislature is free to legislate to give effect to that decision.

ADOPTION

In an adoption, the natural parents of a child give up their rights and duties over that child to the adoptive parent(s) to whom the child then stands as if it had been born to them. Adoption creates a permanent legal relationship between the adoptive parents and the child. As adoption is for the benefit of children, the welfare of the child is the first and paramount consideration in any adoption matter.

Generally, Adoption Societies and Health Boards place children for adoption and then the Adoption Board, a statutory body appointed by government, makes or refuses to make an adoption order, the final decision in the whole process. The Adoption Board is composed of a chairperson and six ordinary members.

In Ireland, adoption was not provided for in law until 1953. Since then, over 37,000 adoption orders have been made.

Who may be Adopted?

Orphans and non-marital children, resident in the state, who are over six weeks of age and under eighteen years. Children over seven years must have their wishes considered. In exceptional circumstances, the High Court may authorise the adoption of children whose parents have failed in their duty towards them. The child need not have been born in this country.

Who may Adopt?

A validly married couple who are living together, the mother, natural father, a relative of the child, e.g. a grandparent, a widow or widower. Should any other person wish to adopt a child, if the

Adoption Board is satisfied that it is desirable in the particular circumstances of the case an adoption order may be made in favour of such person.

Generally, prospective adopters must have reached twenty-one years of age. Where the applicants are a married couple both must be twenty-one years old, except where one partner is the mother, father or a relative of the child, in which case only one partner must have reached twenty-one years of age.

The adopting parents must be ordinarily resident in the state, be of good moral character, have sufficient means to support the child and be suitable candidates for parenthood. An applicant will have to undergo a detailed assessment process. In addition to the various screening procedures used by the adoption agencies, the Adoption Board carries out its own assessment. An Adoption Board social worker makes at least two visits to the applicant's home. Adopting parents usually have the child in their care for at least six months before an adoption is finalised. Prior to the granting of the order there is an oral hearing before the Board where the applicants are asked questions, on oath, to establish their suitability to adopt.

Whose Consent is Required?
The mother's or guardian's clear consent is required to the adoption. The consent of the natural father is required if he marries the natural mother after the birth of the child; if he is appointed a guardian of the child; or if he is granted custody of the child. The consent must be freely given. It must not be the product of fear, anxiety or duress.

The Adoption Board may dispense with such consent where the person is incapable of giving it through mental disability or because he/she cannot be found.

Birth Certificates
When an adoption order is made, a new 'birth' certificate may be obtained for the child. This is not an actual birth certificate but is a certified copy of the entry relating to the child in the Adopted Children Register. The long form of the certificate gives the date of the adoption order and the name(s) and address of the adoptive parent(s).

Foreign Adoptions
The Adoption Act, 1991 was introduced primarily to regularise

foreign adoptions. Prior to the passing of this Act, such adoptions were in a legal limbo. Now, as in the case of any prospective adopters, those wishing to travel abroad to adopt must have their suitability and eligibility established before they travel.

After an initial assessment by the local Health Board, the proposed adopter(s) may apply through the Health Board or a registered adoption society to the Adoption Board for a formal declaration of their suitability and eligibility to adopt. This declaration will be required in order to get Department of Justice permission to bring a child into the country. The declaration and the assessment report can be presented to foreign adoption authorities as evidence that they have been approved for an inter-country adoption by the Irish authorities.

Information
Adopted children in the Republic of Ireland have no legal rights to information about their natural parents. In Northern Ireland in 1990, adopted children were granted the right to obtain copies of their original birth certificate. Such a right already exists in England, Scotland and Wales.

Wills
Adoptive parents should be careful when making their wills; it would be prudent to take legal advice. A High Court decision (August 1992) has determined that the word 'issue' in a will means children related by blood, thus excluding adopted children.

A farmer who died in 1954 had included a provision in his will that if his son should 'die without leaving issue' the property should be left in trust to a grandson. The son married and adopted two children and these two children were denied the right to inherit their father's farm because the word 'issue' was used in the will. Had the term 'child' been used, the result would have been quite different.

Adoption and Maternity Leave
Under the Maternity (Protection of Employees) Act, 1981 a woman who is employed for twenty-six weeks (or under a fixed term contract for less), and is insured for social welfare, is entitled to ten weeks' leave when she adopts a child.

ANNULMENT

When discussing nullity it is essential to draw a distinction between a civil or state annulment and a church annulment. Many people think that, simply because they have a church annulment, their marriage no longer exists in the eyes of the law. This is not the case. A church annulment is a church annulment; it does not affect one's legal status.

What is a civil/state annulment? An annulment (Decree of Nullity) is a declaration by the High Court that an apparently validly contracted marriage is in fact null and void. It never existed. The couple involved are in the same position as if they had never married. Rights to maintenance and inheritance are affected. If there are children, the father may cease to be guardian of those children. The mother would generally be entitled to apply for Unmarried Mothers Allowance in respect of any children. There are also tax implications. A person seeking an annulment must take their case to the High Court. As the law in this area is quite complex, legal advice is essential.

A marriage may be annulled for any of the following reasons:

   (1) Lack of capacity. If either party is at the time already married to another then the ceremony has no legal effect as s/he is not capable of marrying. If either party was under sixteen years and did not have the consent of the High Court to marry; or if the parties were closely related or of the same sex, then there is also incapacity to marry.

   (2) Non-observance of the formalities. In some situations disregarding the procedures or formalities necessary for a valid marriage may make such marriage invalid. For example, a marriage is invalid if there are no witnesses.

   (3) Absence of consent. As a marriage is a voluntary union, here must be full and free consent to it. There are a number of circumstances where consent may be lacking:

   (a) *Insanity.* If it can be proved that, at the time of the ceremony, one person was incapable of understanding the implications of a marriage contract through insanity, then that marriage may be annulled.

   (b) *Intoxication.* If, at the time of the ceremony, either party was so drunk as to be incapable of knowing what s/he was doing, then the marriage may be annulled.

   (c) *Duress.* If a person is forced to go through a marriage ceremony by fear, threats or pressure etc., such a marriage may be annulled. What amounts to duress depends on the particular circumstances in each case. Duress may be imposed by one of the parties to the marriage or by someone else. Examples of where annulments have been granted on this ground:

- where a marriage was arranged (1965), because of the pregnancy, for a 16-year-old pregnant girl. She had not been advised on alternatives such as adoption or bringing up the child as a single parent.
- where a woman induced a man into marriage by falsely claiming she was pregnant by him and by threatening that if he did not marry her she would bring legal proceedings against him.

(d) *Impotence.* If, at the time of the marriage, either party was impotent, the Court may grant an annulment. Impotence is the inability to consummate the marriage, i.e. to engage in normal sexual intercourse. Impotence may be caused by physical factors or by psychological factors. The impotence need not be absolute. It need only be relative to the other spouse. The fact that either party may be able to have sexual intercourse with other people is irrelevant.

(e) *Inability* to sustain a normal marital relationship. This is a new ground upon which the courts will grant an annulment. The disability in question may be psychological, emotional or psychiatric. It must have existed at the time of the marriage and must not have been known to the party seeking the annulment. Needless to say, the disability must be of a serious nature. Examples of situations where courts granted annulments for this reason:

- where there was gross immaturity of personality.
- where one party was diagnosed as paranoid / schizophrenic.
  The court did emphasise however that not every schizophrenic would be incapable of sustaining a normal marital relationship.
- the incapacity of one of the parties to form or maintain a normal marital relationship by virtue of an inherent and unalterable homosexual nature.

ARREST

An arrest is the apprehension of a person for the purpose of bringing that person to justice before a court. Gardaí have wide powers of arrest both at common law and under various acts. Private citizens also have powers of arrest but, in practice, they are not frequently used.

Powers of arrest come from three sources:
(1) The Common Law
(2) Legislation
(3) Warrants to arrest

(1) The Common Law

This is one of the earliest sources of Irish law predating both legislation and the Constitution. It comprises court decisions called precedents which are applied in similar subsequent cases making for a certain consistency in the application of law.

Under common law a garda must arrest a person s/he sees committing
- treason
- a felony (serious offences such as larceny, murder, etc.)
- a dangerous wounding
- a breach of the peace which cannot otherwise be prevented; breach of the peace means harm done, or likely to be, to a person or his/her property by means of an assault or unlawful assembly.

A garda may arrest a person whom s/he reasonably suspects of having committed, or being about to commit, any of the above or who assaults or obstructs the garda in the execution of his/her duty.

A private citizen may arrest any person s/he reasonably suspects of having committed:
- treason
- a felony
- a dangerous wounding

provided that such crime was actually committed. When a citizen's arrest is made the person detained must be handed over to a garda as soon as possible. Due caution should be observed when exercising this right of arrest. By arresting the wrong person it is possible that a civil action could ensue for assault, battery, false imprisonment and defamation. Mistakes can be expensive. These arrests are carried out without warrants.

(2) Legislation

Various Acts grant a power of arrest without warrant (usually to a garda). What follows are *some* examples of situations where such power may be exercised.

Betting Act, 1931

– a bookmaker who refuses to produce a licence for inspection.

Casual Trading Act, 1980

– casual trading without the required permit/licence or trading in a manner inconsistent with the conditions set out in a permit. Goods involved may be seized and sold to cover the cost of seizure, storage, etc. Casual trading means selling goods in a public place such as a road, street or market. It *does not* include the selling of farm produce by a farmer, selling to a person at his/her home or business, selling sweets, cooked foods, soft drinks or fruit at public events, selling ice-cream, papers or religious objects, selling fish from a boat, selling goods where the entire profits are for charitable use and *no* payment is made to the seller.

Criminal Justice Act, 1951

– where a garda has a reasonable suspicion that a person has stolen goods in his/her possession.

Criminal Justice Act, 1960

– where a garda suspects a person is at large, who is either an escaped convict or one who has failed to answer bail.

Criminal Law (Jurisdiction) Act, 1979

– where there is reasonable cause to suspect a person of committing an offence in Northern Ireland which, if committed here, would be a 'scheduled offence' under the Act.

Scheduled offences include

- murder
- manslaughter
- arson
- kidnapping
- malicious damage
- making, possessing explosives
- causing an explosion
- robbery
- possessing, using a firearm
- hijacking

– where there is reasonable cause to suspect a person of escape (after charge or conviction for any of the scheduled offences) from lawful custody in Northern Ireland. A citizen may make the arrest, provided that the offence was actually committed or attempted. A garda may arrest if s/he suspects that they have been committed or are about to be committed.

Criminal Law (Sexual Offences) Act, 1993

– where a garda reasonably suspects that a person has committed certain offences under the Act. These offences include committing an act of gross indecency with another male under the age of seventeen years and soliciting for the purposes of prostitution.

Defence Act, 1954

– a person who is reasonably suspected of being an army deserter. Any officer, man (i.e., a member of the Defence Forces who is not an officer) or garda may make the arrest.

Under the Dublin Police Acts

– any person who, in the presence of a garda, puts notices on buildings without the owner's consent, sells obscene literature, sings obscene songs or uses obscene language to the annoyance of the public, discharges a gun, throws a stone thereby endangering any person, makes a bonfire, lets off fireworks, rings doorbells, knocks at doors without lawful excuse, slides on ice in a street and endangers passers-by, is drunk and disorderly in a public place within the Dublin Police District.

Prevention of Electoral Abuses Act, 1923

– a person who commits the offence of personation or who is believed (by the garda) to have committed it.

– where the returning officer or any presiding officer reasonably suspects that a person has committed the offence or is committing it s/he may, before that person leaves the polling station, direct a garda to arrest such a person.

Family Law (Protection of Spouses and Children) Act, 1981

– a spouse who contravenes a barring order or a protection order. Attempting to enter the family home or being in the vicinity of the family home or other place where the protected spouse and children live, constitutes a breach of a barring order.

Firearms and Offensive Weapons Act, 1990

– any person committing the following offences or who, with reasonable cause, is suspected of committing such offences: possessing in a public place a knife or other sharply pointed article without good reason (i.e. for use at work or for a recreational purpose); possessing a flick-knife in a public place without good reason; possessing in a public place any article intended to intimidate or cause injury; trespassing in a premises while possessing a knife or other article adapted to cause injury.

Prohibition of Forcible Entry and Occupation Act, 1971

– a person who without right forcibly occupies a house or land or vehicle. To occupy forcibly means to prevent others from entering lawfully, e.g. by erecting obstructions.

Larceny Act, 1916

– a person who carries off without right anything which is capable of being stolen (i.e. which has value and belongs to another) with the intent of depriving the owner of it
– stealing goods, money, etc. from a person, house, boat, dock, vessel in distress, etc.
– fraudulently using or diverting electricity
– trustees, directors converting property to their own use
– receiving or handling stolen property
– robbery (larceny with force or threatened force)
– burglary.

A citizen also has the right to make arrests in all these situations.

Liquor Licensing Laws

– a person who is drunk and in charge of a child apparently under seven years.
– 'found ons' who refuse to give names and addresses or give what a garda has grounds to believe are false names and addresses. A 'found on' is a person found on a licensed premises after hours.
– a person found drunk in a public place.

Malicious Damage Act, 1861

– any person found pulling down or destroying a church, house, farm, building, workplace, shed, public building, etc. in a riot
– unlawfully breaking or uprooting trees, shrubs, etc. in a park or near a dwelling
– unlawfully interfering with railways, e.g. removing sleepers, points, etc.
– unlawfully and maliciously wounding or killing cattle
– unlawfully and maliciously pulling down bridges or quays.

Any person found committing an offence under this Act may be arrested by a garda, the owner of the property or the owner's agent. A garda may arrest any person found loitering at night whom s/he with reason suspects is about to commit or has committed a felony under this Act. All of the above are felonies.

Mental Treatment Act, 1945
- a person believed to be of unsound mind may be taken into custody to a police station by a garda if s/he believes such action is necessary for the safety of the public or of the person himself. A recommendation must then be sought by the garda from a registered medical practitioner.

Misuse of Drugs Acts, 1977, 1984
- where a garda with reasonable cause believes that a person has in his/her possession a controlled drug for the purpose of selling or supplying it to another. There are over 125 'controlled' drugs.
- where with reasonable cause a garda suspects that other drug offences have been attempted or committed and that arrest is necessary because the suspect may abscond, does not live in this state or because there are doubts as to his/her identity or place of abode.

Offences Against the Person Act, 1861
- where a person is found loitering at night and a garda has good reason to suspect that that person has committed or is about to commit a felony under this Act, e.g. an attempt to murder, strangle, poison, procure an abortion, etc.

Offences Against the State Act, 1939
- any person suspected of having committed, being about to commit, being concerned in the commission, carrying a document or having information about the commission or intended commission of an offence under this Act. Offences include
- membership of an illegal organisation.
- obstructing the President by violent means in the carrying out of his/her duties.
- preventing or attempting to prevent, by force, the government or any part of it from carrying out its duties.
- scheduled offences include:
  - murder
  - arson
  - kidnapping
  - possessing, using a firearm
  - malicious damage.

Prohibition of Incitement to Hatred Act, 1989
- where a person is reasonably suspected of using words or behaviour which is abusive or threatening and is likely to stir up hatred against a group on account of their race, colour, religion, membership of the travelling community or sexual orientation.

Road Traffic Acts

- drunken driving (driving or attempting to drive a motor vehicle in a public place though incapable through drugs or alcohol).
- being drunk while in charge of a motor vehicle with intent to drive.
- being drunk while in charge of, driving, or attempting to drive a bicycle or animal drawn vehicle.
- being in charge of a motor vehicle while incapable through drugs and refusing to accompany a garda to a Garda Station.
- failing or refusing to give a breath sample.
- dangerous driving (i.e. posing a serious risk to the public).
- unlawfully interfering with or attempting to get on or into a motor vehicle. This does not apply in situations where reasonable steps are taken to move a vehicle which is obstructing a person's way in or out of a place.
- taking a motor vehicle without the owner's consent or being carried knowingly in such vehicle.
- refusing to give a name and address or giving what the garda reasonably believes to be a false name and address.
- being so drunk or drugged in a public place as to be a danger to traffic or oneself.

Street and House to House Collections Act, 1962

- collecting in a street or door to door for a cause charitable or otherwise without a permit (religious denominations are excluded).

Street Trading Act, 1926

- street trading without a certificate authorising such trading.
- refusing to move on from a particular area.

Video Recordings Act, 1989

- failing or refusing to give one's name and address where a garda with reason believes that an offence has been committed under this Act, e.g. supplying videos unlawfully.

(3) Warrants to Arrest

A garda swears an information, that is, he gives a written information on oath to a District Court Judge. On the basis of that information (a copy of which is held in the District Court) the judge issues a warrant or decides that the matter should proceed by way of a summons.

(*See* Bringing a Person before a Court)

ASSAULT

An assault is a violent and unlawful attack on another person. The penalties vary depending on the seriousness of the assault.

For *common assault* the maximum penalty is six months' imprisonment and/or a £50 fine on summary conviction (District Court) or one year's imprisonment on indictment (Circuit Court).

An assault *occasioning actual bodily harm* carries the maximum penalty of one year's imprisonment on summary conviction or five years' imprisonment on indictment. 'Actual bodily harm' means any injury calculated to interfere with the health or comfort of the victim. It includes injury to the mind or body of the victim, e.g. broken nose or nervous condition. The injury need not be of a permanent nature.

The more serious assault which *wounds* or causes *grievous bodily harm,* with or without a weapon, carries a penalty of penal servitude for five years. If a weapon, e.g. a gun, is involved the penalty may be higher. Where the victim is a garda acting in the due execution of his duty the maximum penalty is two years' imprisonment.

(*See* TRESPASS)

BAIL

Bail is the releasing of an accused person from custody subject to the main condition that s/he will turn up for trial. A sum of money (the amount cannot be excessive) is pledged guaranteeing that court appearance. If the accused fails to turn up for trial the sum of money is forfeited to the state and a warrant for arrest is issued. As part of a bail agreement an accused may be asked not to leave the state, to report to a police station regularly, surrender his/her passport, not to associate with certain people and not to visit a particular place or locality.

The concept of bail is based on the presumption in law that a person is innocent until proven guilty. Generally it is only when an accused is convicted by a court that s/he may be deprived of liberty. There are some exceptions to this, however. In certain circumstances a person may be detained for questioning, or remanded in custody where bail has been refused. The Supreme Court in a 1988 case examined the grounds on which bail may be granted and in this judgment reaffirmed an earlier (1966) decision. The probability of the accused evading justice by not turning up for trial or by interfering with witnesses or jurors determines the granting or withholding of bail. The likelihood of further crimes being committed by the accused while on bail is not sufficient reason for denying bail. If further crimes are committed a court has the power to impose consecutive sentences for those offences.

Bail can be granted by a Peace Commissioner, senior garda or a court.

If a person released on bail fails to appear in court in accordance with his bail agreement s/he is guilty of an offence which is punishable by a fine (maximum £1000) or imprisonment for up to twelve months.

BARRING AND PROTECTION ORDERS

Protection Order

This is an Order prohibiting a spouse from using or threatening to use violence against the other spouse or child. This type of order does not require a spouse to leave the home. A Protection Order is a means of getting immediate protection while, perhaps, a Barring Order is being sought although it is of itself very often sufficient to meet the needs of a particular family situation.

Protection Orders may be sought in the District Court or the Circuit Court. It is made on an ex parte basis which simply means that the 'other side' is not aware of the matter unless and until it is granted against him or her. Proceedings are held in camera i.e. in the absence of the public.

Barring Order

This is an Order directing one spouse to leave the place where the other spouse is living or, if they aren't living together, not to enter or go near the place where the other spouse is living. This place may or may not be the family home.

A court must be satisfied that either the applicant spouse or the children (if any) has suffered serious mental or physical cruelty before an order is granted. It can never be granted on the sole grounds that a marriage has irretrievably broken down.

Barring Orders may be sought in the District Court or the Circuit Court. An Order from the District Court lasts for up to one year while a Circuit Court Order lasts indefinitely.

The procedure in the District Court is fairly straightforward. A document known as a summons is taken out in the District Court office and is sent to the other spouse. It states the date, time and place that the case will be heard. On the day, the proceedings are held in camera, with only the couple, their legal representatives, witnesses, the District Justice and a court clerk in attendance. If the order is granted, a copy will be kept at the applicant's local Garda Station so that if it is broken a speedy arrest and charge will be facilitated. A spouse may appeal to the Circuit Court against the granting of a barring order. Where an order has been granted and a spouse breaks it, s/he may be fined up to £200 and/or sent to prison for up to six months.

Applying for an order in a Circuit Court is a little more complicated than in the District Court and legal representation is advisable. A Circuit Court barring order lasts indefinitely. If an offending spouse wishes to have such an order discharged, s/he must apply to the Court and satisfy that court that s/he should be allowed to return to the family home.

Two points worth noting about these orders:
(1) They are open *only* to spouses, i.e. married partners. Unmarried partners in violent relationships must either resort to seeking an injunction (an expensive process) or having the offending partner prosecuted for assault.
(2) Though the safety and welfare of children may be the reason for the granting of these orders, children do not have the power to apply for them.

BIGAMY

If a person, who is validly married, goes through a marriage ceremony with another, s/he is committing the crime of bigamy; it is the only crime that cannot be committed by an unmarried person.

With the absence of divorce in the Republic of Ireland, there are only *three* situations where a person who has married is free to marry again:
(1) where that person is widowed;
(2) where a civil court (in this situation, the High Court) has granted an Annulment, that is, a declaration that the 'first' marriage never existed;
(3) where a valid foreign divorce has been granted.

As many couples go through a Catholic Church annulment process, it is important to point out that such a procedure does not affect one's legal status. You are still legally married. Remarrying after a Church annulment is a crime and though rarely prosecuted in this state there are other serious consequences which should be considered. They are:

(1) The second 'marriage' is void and the parties to it are, in law, co-habitees, i.e. living together.

(2) It is a crime and a prosecution may result though, as stated above, this rarely happens. The penalty is seven years' penal servitude or two years' imprisonment. The other party to this bigamous marriage may also be prosecuted but as an aider and abettor.

(3) The parties have no automatic right to inherit from each other.

(4) The parties are not obliged to maintain each other. However, if there are children, the mother can apply for maintenance from the father for that child or children. This may involve proving paternity.

(5) They cannot claim social welfare payments as a married couple.

(6) They cannot be treated as a married couple for income tax or Capital Acquisitions Tax purposes.

(7) The Family Home Protection Act, which prevents the sale of the family home without the written consent of both spouses, cannot be invoked.

(8) The Family Law (Protection of Spouses and Children) Act, which established barring orders, cannot be invoked. Therefore, if a person finds himself or herself in a violent relationship, the only legal remedies are an injunction, which can be costly both in time and money, or a prosecution for assault.

BIRTH CERTIFICATES

Birth Certificates contain the following information: date and place of birth, name, sex, name and place of residence of father, father's occupation and mother's name.

The hospital where the child was born normally registers the birth. Proper registration is vitally important as birth certificates are essential at various stages of a child's life e.g. school enrolment, commencing employment, obtaining passports, applying for social welfare benefits, etc.

If the parents are not married to each other, the hospital may only register the name of the mother. To have the name and occupation of the father included in the Birth Register the following options are open:
- both parents may attend at the Registrar's office and jointly sign the Register;
- either parent may complete a Declaration Form and attend at the Registrar's office bringing a Statutory Declaration by the other parent;
- either parent may register the birth on production to the Registrar of a certified copy of a court order in respect of proceedings to which Section 45 of the Status of Children Act, 1987 relates, naming the person to be registered as the father. According to Section 45, if a person is adjudged to be a parent of a child in guardianship or maintenance proceedings, etc. then that is proof of parentage for any subsequent proceedings.

Stillborn Children
The legal definition of stillbirth is the death of a baby after twenty-eight weeks of pregnancy. In Ireland, there are more than 400 stillbirths every year. Such births are not registered. All other EC member states have an official stillbirth register entitling parents to birth and death certificates. There is no stillbirth register in this state, such lack of official recognition being a source of added grief to many in an all too tragic situation.

BRINGING A PERSON BEFORE A COURT
One of two procedures may be used by the state to bring a person before a court to answer a criminal charge. They are by means of (1) a summons or (2) arrest and charge.

Summons
This is a document served on an accused person informing him or her of the nature of the complaint which has been made (e.g. failure to produce a TV licence, assault, etc.) and requiring him or her to attend court on a specified date and time to answer the charge. The court appearance will generally be some weeks away so that the accused will have time to arrange legal representation and prepare a defence. The prosecution will have time to prepare

its case, get witness statements, forensic reports, a book of evidence, etc. This procedure is used for most motoring offences and matters that are considered minor. However, it is capable of being used for more serious offences and is often used in respect of serious fraud and manslaughter.

Arrest and Charge

This is a procedure whereby a suspect is arrested by one or more gardaí and taken to a police station to be charged. At the time of the arrest he will be informed in general terms of the nature of the crime alleged against him and cautioned that anything he says may be used in evidence. He will then be taken into custody to a police station where the charge will be read over to him formally. He will be given a legal caution and informed of his rights while in custody. His reply will later be given in evidence. A custody record will then be opened on him. There is a legal obligation to bring him before a court as soon as practicable, which is usually the next day. The period between arrest and his appearance in court will be taken up with various procedures. These will usually involve a search, having his property taken, finger-printing, tests for forensic examination, etc., but it must be stressed that the nature and extent of these procedures will be determined by the reason for the arrest.

BUSINESS NAMES

There is no legal impediment to any person or group of persons who wish to carry on business. However, if such person or group of persons choose to carry on a business in a name other than their own they are obliged to register this fact under the Registration of Business Names Act. They must register within one month from the commencement of trading under a name other than their own. This will be done by completing a form and lodging it in the Companies Office Registration of Business Names Section, Dublin Castle, Dublin 2. When this form has been lodged the Registrar of Business Names will issue a Certificate of Registration which must be exhibited in the principal place of business of the particular people. It should also be noted that the Minister for Enterprise and Employment may refuse to allow the registration of any name which, in his opinion, is undesirable. There is a right of appeal to the High Court from such a decision by the Minister.

CHILDREN

What is a child? In Ireland a child, or minor, is any person who has not yet reached eighteen years of age. In that eighteen-year span it is worth noting that various stages are of legal significance. For example an infant must be at least six weeks old before he can be adopted. At seven years of age he may be sued.

The age of criminal responsibility is also seven years of age so he may be prosecuted. However in the case of minors between seven and fourteen years of age it is necessary not alone to prove that the minor committed the crime but also that he knew that what he was doing was wrong. There used to be an irrefutable presumption that a boy under the age of fourteen years was incapable of committing rape but that was removed by the Criminal Law (Rape) Act, 1990.

At sixteen years of age a minor may marry. At eighteen years he has the capacity to enter legally binding contracts with other persons. He may vote in elections at eighteen years of age but may not put himself forward as a candidate until he is twenty-one years of age in the case of the Dáil and Seanad, and thirty-five years of age for the office of President.

Abandonment

Abandoning or exposing a child under two years so that its health is endangered is an offence for which the penalty is five years' penal servitude.

Child Abduction

Unlawfully taking a child under fourteen years by force, fraud or persuasion with intent to deprive a parent or guardian of the possession of such a child is an offence punishable by up to seven years' penal servitude.

The force or fraud may be employed against either the child or the parent or guardian.

Cruelty

Any person over seventeen years who has custody, charge or care of a child or young person and assaults, ill-treats, neglects or causes it to be so ill-treated is guilty of an offence for which the penalty is on indictment £100 or two years' imprisonment or on summary conviction £25 or six months' imprisonment (*see also* TRESPASS).

Tug-of-love Cases

The incidence of this type of situation is quite low in Ireland. However, it is not inconceivable that an estranged partner, for instance, might attempt to remove his/her child from the care of the former partner. What can be done legally to prevent this? There are a number of possibilities depending on whether the child has been taken to another place within the country or taken abroad.

If a child is still in the country, a custody order should be applied for and *(i)* an order for the production of the child (usually within one or two days) or *(ii)* a habeas corpus order.

If there is a fear that a child may be removed from the country then *(i)* an order prohibiting the removal of the child from the jurisdiction without the parent's and/or court's consent, or *(ii)* an injunction prohibiting the removal of the child (Circuit or High Court order) should be sought.

In such cases a court will also authorise the notification of the Commissioner of the Gardaí and all points of exit from the country of the details of the order.

A garda may detain a child whom he reasonably suspects is about to be removed from the state in breach of a custody order, access order etc. and have him/her placed in the care of a person or place nominated by a court.

What can be done where a child has been taken abroad? The Child Abduction and Enforcement of Custody Orders Act, 1991 provides a mechanism whereby a person in this state can seek the return of an abducted child or have custody and related orders enforced in another contracting state. Persons in other countries have reciprocal powers in relation to abducted children who have been brought here. Applications may be brought to a court (generally the High Court or its equivalent), the Minister for Justice, or the Central Authority which is a body specially appointed by the Justice Minister to deal with these matters. Steps can then be taken to return children who have been abducted or to enforce custody or access and related orders in respect of these children.

This Act has its origins in two 1980 conventions: the Hague Convention on Child Abduction and the Luxembourg Convention on Custody of Children.

COMMUNITY SERVICE ORDER

A community service order is an alternative to a custodial sentence. It may be imposed where the offender is sixteen years of age or more and a court is satisfied, having considered probation and welfare officers' reports, that it is an appropriate form of punishment for that offender.

Under an order an offender is required to perform unpaid work for a specified number of hours not less than forty and not more than 240. Generally, the work must be performed within a period of a year though in certain circumstances this may be extended. The hours of work under this order should not interfere with an offender's course of study or employment.

COMPANY LAW
What is a Company?

The law regards a company as a person just like any human being. It can own property, have a bank account, it can own machinery, it can be owed money, it can owe money, it can employ people to work, it can enter into contracts. The company's money and property belong to the company and not to the shareholders. In a similar manner a company's debts are the debts of the company and not the debts of the shareholders. It must be stressed that the concept of the company as a separate person, distinct from shareholders and directors, is the fundamental principle of company law. As a human is born, lives a life and eventually dies, a company is incorporated, trades and in all likelihood will eventually be wound up at some time. Unlike a human a company can of course go on forever.

Types of Companies

The common types of companies are as follows:

(1) A company limited by shares. In this case the liability of a shareholder to contribute to the company's assets is limited to the amount, if any, unpaid on his shares. For example, if he purchases a share worth £10 and pays £8 the amount unpaid is £2. In the event of the company going into liquidation he will be liable personally for £2.

(2) A company limited by guarantee. In this case liability of a member is limited to the amount which he has undertaken to contribute in the event of the company being wound up.

It can be a public or a private company formed with or without a share capital, although normally it is formed without a share capital. This type of company usually deals with professional trade, tenants' associations and clubs.

(3) An unlimited company. As the name suggests the liability of the member is unlimited.

How does a Company come into Being?

The process is called incorporation. To incorporate a company certain documents must be lodged with the Registrar of Companies, Dublin Castle. The principal documemnts are a Memorandum of Association, a set of Articles of Association, statement of the nominal share capital, and a declaration of Compliance with the requirements of the Companies Acts. This declaration is usually made by the solicitor engaged in the formation of the company.

A Memorandum of Association is the constitution of a company, setting out its objects. These objects define the powers of the company, which may not carry on any business unprovided for in the objects clause of the Memorandum of Association. Any such transaction would be *ultra vires,* that is beyond the power of the company. The Memorandum of Association also sets out the share capital of the company and the division to which the shares are to be fixed - for example, a share capital of £100 divided into one hundred shares of £1 each.

The Articles of Association are, in effect, the rules of the company and set out how it goes about its business. They generally deal with meetings of shareholders, directors' powers, the extent to which directors can delegate their power to a managing director and, of course, the dividends.

Statement of the Nominal Share Capital is self-evident and is merely a statement of the amount of capital with which a company nominally intends to trade. This remains nominal until such time as the shares are issued. In the ordinary everyday company normally no more than two shares are issued. These are generally to the principal entrepreneur himself and a member of his family. So in the example above of a company having a share capital of £100 divided into one hundred shares of £1 each normally two shares will be issued and 98 shares will remain unissued.

Declaration by a solicitor engaged in the formation of a company is, like the statement of nominal share capital, self-evident. The solicitor, or a member of the company who makes the declaration, swears that everything is in order.

Membership of a company occurs when a share is issued to you. What does this share mean? A share has been defined as 'the interest of a shareholder in a company measured by a sum of money, for the purpose of liability in the first place, and of interest in the second place, but also consisting of a series of mutual covenants entered into by all the shareholders between themselves'. A share in a company is what is known as personal property and is transferable in the manner provided by the Articles of the Company. On becoming a member of a company one is normally issued with a share certificate. If you cease to be a member and wish to transfer your share, you merely hand over the share certificate and a share transfer form to the person who is buying the share from you. That person will then send the share transfer form for noting to the company secretary who will alter the Register of Shareholders. This Register is normally held by the company secretary at the registered office of the company. As stated above the shares are personal property and may be mortgaged by the holder. A private company must have at least two shareholders and a public company must have at least seven shareholders.

Directors

These are the people to whom the running of the company is normally entrusted, normally a small group. In a private company they are likely to be the same as the shareholders and would certainly include one of the substantial shareholders. In a public company they may be shareholders but their principal source of reward from the company will be the fees they are paid for their directorships. In a public company the appointment of directors always takes place at a general meeting and must be voted on individually unless a resolution to the contrary has been first agreed to without any vote being given against it. The powers of directors depends on the articles of association. So it is absolutely essential that directors carry out their functions within the limits laid down by these articles. The law places very stringent duties on directors. They owe what is called a fiduciary duty to the company but not to the individual members or to anyone else. A fiduciary duty means that the directors must exercise their powers *bona fide* for the purpose for which they are conferred, in short for the benefit of the company. They must also not put themselves in a position where their duties and their personal interest may conflict. Another aspect of this fiduciary duty is that a director may not make a secret profit out of his position. Should a director make such a profit he must account for it to the company.

The Secretary

The secretary is involved in the administration of the company. The secretary can be a shareholder, a director or may not be a member of the company at all. As such a secretary does not have any power to bind a company. However, it is established that a secretary is the proper official to issue a share certificate. In particular the secretary is expected to attend to the following matters:

(a) Keeping a register of members, a register of directors and secretaries, register of debentures and a register of director shareholdings.

(b) Making the annual return to the Registrar of Companies.

(c) Keeping minutes of general meetings and of meetings of board of directors.

(d) Notifying the Companies Office of any alterations in the Memorandum and Articles of Association.

(e) Giving notice of meetings.

(f) Furnishing the Companies Office with particulars of any charges entered into by the company and also with the discharge of any charges entered into by the company. He must be named in a statement that has to be delivered to the Registrar of Companies.

Meetings

There are principally three types of meetings by which the members of a company exercise their control over the company. These are:

(a) The annual general meeting;

(b) Extraordinary general meeting; and

(c) A separate meeting of classes of shareholders.

Annual General Meeting

Every company, be it public or private, must hold an annual general meeting. Not less than fifteen months may elapse between the date of holding one general meeting and the next. The first annual general meeting must be held within eighteen months of the date of incorporation of the company. A meeting will generally review the year's business and will, in addition, deal with a declaration of a dividend if one is to be made, the election of directors, the appointment of and retirement of auditors and the remuneration of directors and auditors.

Extraordinary General Meeting

Under a power given by Section 132 of the Companies Act, 1963 whereby the members may convene a general meeting even if the directors do not wish to have one. Members of the company seeking such a meeting must state the object of the meeting in writing and deposit such requisition at the registered office of the company. If the directors do not convene a meeting within twenty-one days of the requisition being deposited the people seeking the extraordinary general meeting may convene it themselves. Unless the articles provide to the contrary, voting at all meetings is by a show of hands. Each member present is entitled to one vote only irrespective of the number of shares that member holds.

Prospectuses

These arise when the public is asked to subscribe for shares or debentures in a company. This involves the issue of a document setting out the advantages to accrue from an investment in a company. This particular document is termed a prospectus. A prospectus will set out:

    (a) Who the directors are and what benefit they get from their directorships;

    (b) What profit is being made by the promoters;

    (c) The amount of capital required by the company to be subscribed;

    (d) The company's financial record;

    (e) What the company's obligations are under contracts which have already been entered into;

    (f) What the voting and dividend rights of each class of share a person proposing to invest in the company will have. The investor will have to rely on the accuracy of a prospectus and accordingly the person preparing the prospectus must be very careful. The leading case in this area is that of *Derry* v. *Peek* (1889). In this case a tramway company had, by special Act of Parliament, the power to drive its trams by animal power and—with the consent of the Board of Trade—by steam power. The directors issued a prospectus stating

simply that the company had the right to run trams driven by steam power. Peek's subscribed for shares on the strength of this prospectus and when the Board of Trade refused its consent the company went into liquidation. Peek, who suffered financially as a result, sued for fraud. It was held by the House of Lords that the directors had acted honestly in the belief that the statement in the prospectus was true, and they were therefore not liable to him.

Allotment

The ordinary law of contract applies to an agreement to take shares in a company. However, where a prospectus is issued by a company the prospectus is not an offer, rather it is an invitation to the public to make offers. The offer is made by the applicant in sending in a formal application for shares to the company and it is accepted by the allotment of shares to the applicant. Normally, the power to allot shares is vested in the board of directors.

Dividends

A dividend is the share of the company's profit legally available to be divided among its members. In the normal situation it is the shareholders' entitlement to a share of the profits of the company. However, it is a fundamental principle of company law that dividends may not be paid out of the capital, as capital must be spent on the objects defined in the memorandum.

Debentures

The word debenture has more commercial than legal significance. It comes from the Latin word *debere* (to owe) and generally means a document given under the seal of a company to secure the repayment of money to a creditor of the company. It is not itself a security. It usually gives a charge on the assets of the company by way of security, although it need not necessarily do so. As you will see a debenture may be secured or it may be unsecured. However, it is always for a specified sum. Debentures secured by a fixed charge on the company's assets are called mortgage debentures.

Fixed Charge

A fixed charge is a mortgage of ascertained definite property. It effectively means that the title to the property is vested in the lender and accordingly that the company may not dispose of the property without first repaying the charge.

Floating Charge

A floating charge does not attach to any particular item of company property but is rather a charge over the company's assets. It remains dormant until such time as there has been a default in the repayments of the charge. The document creating the floating charge will provide for this event; if and when it happens the floating charge will crystallise and become a fixed charge.

Debenture mortgages, fixed charges and floating charges must be notified to the Registrar of Companies within twenty-one days of their creation. If this is not done they may lose out on priority and an application to the High Court to extend time will be necessary.

Winding-up

Winding-up effectively means the death of a company. It may be done by the court or it may be a voluntary winding-up. A company may also cease to exist by being struck off the Register by the Registrar of Companies for failing to deliver any returns. A court winding-up starts by the presentation of a petition to the court to wind up the company. This is usually presented either by the company itself or by a creditor. A notice of the petition to wind up must be published in the newspapers so that all creditors are aware and may attend the petition hearing. This stops a creditor from using a petition to satisfy his own debt while excluding other creditors. To issue a petition for these reasons is an abuse of the court. Once a petition has been presented to the court it is not open to the petitioner to withdraw it. If the petition is accepted the court will appoint a liquidator, who will then basically attend to the winding-up of the company. He will sell all the assets and discharge liabilities to the maximum extent possible. However, when he is paying off creditors he must pay them off in the correct order. Secure creditors obviously come first, followed by preferential creditors - for example the Revenue Commissioners - and finally ordinary creditors.

Voluntary Winding-up

A voluntary winding-up may be either a members' voluntary winding-up or a creditors' voluntary winding-up. A members' voluntary winding-up takes place only when the company is solvent. To effect this type of winding-up the directors must be able to lodge a declaration of solvency. In a creditors' voluntary winding-up no declaration of solvency is required. In this case the company must summon a meeting of the creditors for a day on which a resolution for voluntary winding-up is to be proposed. A notice of the meeting of creditors must be sent to the creditors at the same time as the notice of the meeting is sent to the members of the company. The notice must also be advertised in the paper. The business of such a meeting is normally as follows:

(*a*) To receive a statement by the directors of the position of the company's affairs together with a list of creditors and the estimated amount of claims;

(*b*) To appoint a liquidator;

(*c*) To appoint a committee of inspection.

The liquidator in a voluntary winding-up is not an officer of the court, i.e. he does not have to report back to the court from time to time. The commencement of a voluntary winding-up is the date of passing of the resolution for the winding-up. As and from that date the company must cease to carry on business except so far as it is required for the beneficial winding-up. No transfers of shares can take place without the sanction of the liquidator. On the appointment of the liquidator the powers of the directors cease. The liquidator then normally realises such assets as the company may have and discharges the liabilities in so far as that is possible. Clearly fixed charges and preferential creditors must be paid in advance of unsecured creditors. The costs and expenses incurred in a voluntary winding-up including the remuneration of liquidator are payable in priority to other claims.

Receivers

A receiver is generally appointed under a power contained in a debenture which enables his appointment. He takes possession of the property of the company for which he is appointed and realises it for the benefit of the debenture holder. He should not therefore be confused with a liquidator. On the appointment of a receiver a floating charge will crystallise and become fixed. This stops the company from dealing with the assets so charged without the receiver's consent. On his appointment the directors' power of controlling the company is suspended. They cannot claim remuneration from the receiver unless he employs them. However, they can still claim remuneration from the company. The remuneration of a receiver appointed by a court is normally fixed by the court while the remuneration of a receiver appointed under a power in a debenture is generally fixed by agreement.

Examinership

This concept is new to Irish law. The basic idea behind it is to give a company some breathing time to see if it is possible for it to get out of difficulty and to trade profitably again. An examiner is appointed by the court when it appears that the company is unable to pay its debts. There must be no winding-up order in being or any liquidation. The application may be presented by the company itself, by its directors, by a creditor or by a member holding not less than one-tenth of the voting shares. When the court appoints an examiner the company is deemed to be under the protection of the court. During that period no winding-up can take place, no receiver can be appointed, no secured creditor can take steps to realise his security without the consent of the examiner, goods of the company subject to hire purchase agreements may not be repossessed, and no attachment or execution orders against the company may be enforced. The examiner's duty is to conduct an examination of the company's affairs within twenty-one days or within such longer period as the court will decide. If an examiner comes to the conclusion that the company cannot be got back on the rails he must report so to the court immediately who will convene a hearing to consider the report. In that event it is likely that the court will order a winding-up of the company. This Act was first used in relation to the Goodman companies.

CONSTITUTIONAL RIGHTS

The individual has natural and human rights over which the state has no authority. The fundamental rights or the constitutional rights declared in the constitution are not created by the constitution. If that were so then, by referendum, these rights could be altered. According to Judge Kenny in the celebrated case of *Ryan* v. *Attorney-General* (1965): 'There are many personal rights of the citizens which follow from the Christian and democratic nature of the state which are not mentioned in the constitution.'

It is open to an individual to challenge the operation of a particular Act. The challenge is commenced in the High Court to have the section of the Act made repugnant to the constitution. It is open to the state to appeal the decision of the High Court if it is found that this section is repugnant. If the state does not institute an appeal that section of the Act is no longer valid; it is simply unconstitutional.

It is also open to an individual to seek damages or an injunction for breaches of constitutional rights. Articles 40-44 are viewed as fundamental rights in the constitution and article 40 deals with personal rights. Two sections of article 40 are worthy of note. Article 40.1 states that all citizens shall as human persons be held equal before the law and article 40.4.1 states that no citizen shall be deprived of his personal liberty save in accordance with law.

In the matter of equality before the law, the state may in its laws have regard to the differences of capacity, physical and moral, between citizens. This means that laws must not discriminate invidiously, which is defined as in an arbitrary, unreasonable or unjust manner, between citizens. If a citizen believes that he or she is wrongfully detained, an application for habeas corpus may be made on his or her behalf. If the High Court is satisfied that the detention is unlawful it will order the release of the individual. Successful applications have been made against institutions, against detention by the gardaí, against prison authorities, or as a relief by one parent against another parent where the custody of an infant was in issue.

Article 40.5 states that the dwelling of every citizen is inviolable and shall not be forcibly entered save in accordance with law. Simply put, it is not open to the gardaí to enter a person's house without a valid search warrant.

Article 40 further states that the state guarantees liberty for the exercise of the following rights, subject to public order and morality: the right of the citizens to express freely their convictions and opinions; the right of the citizens to assemble peaceably and without arms; and the right of the citizens to form associations and unions. The right of the citizen to express freely his convictions and opinions must be balanced in such a manner so as not to undermine public order or public morality or the authority of the state. The right to assemble peaceably is subject to public order and morality. The law will not tolerate meetings or assemblies which are likely or calculated to cause a riot or breach of the peace. The fundamental right of the citizen to form associations and unions is in large measure unlimited. The associations may be sporting, social, commercial, political or charitable in nature. Naturally enough, associations or assemblies which might threaten the stability of the state will not be permitted.

Article 41 deals with the family and the state recognises the family as the natural primary and fundamental unit group of society. Furthermore, the state guarantees to protect the family in its constitution and authority as the necessary basis of social order and as indispensable to the welfare of the nation and the state. The right to marry is not expressed in the constitution though it is generally accepted as an implied personal right. In fact, the implied right was exercised by Rose Dugdale and Eddie Gallagher, both of whom were serving prison terms on the day of their marriage.

Article 41.3.2 states that no law should be enacted providing for the grant of a dissolution of marriage. The Minister for Justice has issued a white paper on marital breakdown and an undertaking is given to hold a referendum on divorce after a full public debate on the issues pertaining to property rights of the spouses. A referendum seeking to introduce divorce, held in 1986, was heavily defeated.

Article 42 acknowledges that the primary and natural educator of the child is the family and also states that parents shall be free to provide this education in their homes or in private schools or in schools recognised and established by the state. The same article also indicates that the state shall not oblige parents, in violation of their conscience and lawful preference, to send their children to schools established by the state or to any particular type of school designated by the state. The article dealing with private property acknowledges that man has the natural right to the private ownership of external goods and furthermore the state accordingly guarantees to pass no law attempting to abolish the right of private ownership or the general right to transfer, bequeath and inherit property. The courts have ruled that where any property right is abolished or reduced or restricted, the absence of compensation will make the law invalid because it constitutes an unjust attack on private property rights.

Article 44 allows for freedom to practise religion and the freedom of conscience. However, these rights are subject to public order and morality. The state further guarantees not to endow any particular religion and the property of any religious denomination or educational institution shall not be diverted save where necessary works of public utility and on payment of compensation. The special position of the Roman Catholic Church as originally enshrined in the constitution was deleted by referendum over twenty years ago. Other rights, not specified in the constitution but implied, are: the right to work, the right to earn a livelihood, the right to travel, the right to hold a passport and the right to fair procedures. This is an implied right that has been developed by the courts in recent times.

Only judges may make judgments but tribunals, bodies, agencies and indeed individuals who are not judges make decisions that can have a profound effect upon another individual or body. It is fair to say that the rules of natural justice, developed by the common law, have been adapted by the courts in developing fair procedures. The two most important natural justice rules are: hear the other side and never be a judge in one's own cause. The first one means that a party or individual to be affected by a decision or an adjudication must be given an opportunity to present his or her own side. To do this properly, it is essential that the individual or body be told of the case to be met and be given an opportunity to comment on the case put forward by the opposition. In a celebrated case in the late 1970s, the former commissioner of the Garda Siochana, Mr Garvey, took an action against the state and was successful, because he had been removed from office without being given an opportunity to present his side of the case. Never being a judge in one's own cause is more straightforward. It would be patently unfair and prejudicial if the person who is seeking relief was, in fact, to be part of the decision-making process. The decision that would come from such a tribunal or board would be prejudicial and biased and, in fact, would not conform to the rules of natural justice. The person so affected would have an excellent prospect of having the decisions set aside.

When decisions are made which do not conform to fair procedures and natural justice, the person so affected often avails of judicial review. This is a procedure where an application is made to the court to review or assess the decision made. By availing of judicial review, applicants affected by decisions have effectively reversed those decisions and have been reinstated to the positions that they held prior to the biased or prejudicial decision being made.

Article 28 of the 1937 constitution deals with the government. It declares that nothing in the constitution can invalidate a law enacted by the Oireachtas which is expressly designed to protect public safety and the preservation of the state in time of war or armed rebellion. Nor can the constitution nullify any act done in time of war or armed rebellion in pursuance of such a law.

In this sub-section, time of war includes a time when there is an armed conflict in which the state is not a participant but in respect of which the houses of the Oireachtas shall have resolved that, arising out of such armed conflict, a national emergency exists affecting the vital interests of the state. Time of war or armed rebellion also includes such time after the termination of any war or conflict or armed rebellion as may elapse until each of the houses of the Oireachtas resolve that the national emergency thus occasioned has ceased to exist.

In a state of emergency, *all rights enjoyed and protected by the constitution are, in effect, suspended.* For example, the important right of habeas corpus, which ensures that no citizen shall be deprived of his personal liberty save in accordance with law, is suspended if article 28.3 is called into operation.

Article 28.3 was activated at the outbreak of the Second World War, where the extension of 'the times of war' in article 28.3, to include a war going on in which the state itself was not involved, led to the passing of the Emergency Powers Act, 1939 and of further amendments of it. This gave the executive and the state agencies sweeping powers necessary for the preservation of the state which were immune from constitutional challenge. The Emergency Powers Act, 1939 did not expire until 1946. As a consequence, the written constitution curbing legislative and executive powers was put into suspension.

CONTRACEPTION

By legal definition a contraceptive means any appliance or instrument, excluding contraceptive sheaths, prepared or intended to prevent pregnancy resulting from sexual intercourse between human beings.

Who may Sell Contraceptives?
Chemists (or their employees) in a pharmacy, doctors in a surgery, health board employees at a 'health institution', family planning clinics and hospitals.

Condoms
The Health (Family Planning) (Amendment) Act, 1993 removed

condoms from the list of contraceptive devices and provided for their sale through public vending machines. The Minister for Health has the power to regulate the location of vending machines and to prescribe standards for condoms. The Act also removes any age limit on buying condoms.

Nothing in the family planning acts may be construed as authorising the procuring of abortion or the sale, importation into the state, manufacture, advertising or display of abortifacients.

CONTRACTS

During the course of a day, a person may travel on a bus, travel by taxi, go to a hairdresser, purchase a supply of petrol and, at the end of the day, go into a restaurant and order a meal. All of the above transactions are contracts, even though some of them may have been made unconsciously. Contracts, for that is what they are, intend that their agreement shall be legally binding. These contractual agreements give rise to legal obligations which the law recognises and enforces. But certain agreements such as domestic and social arrangements are not intended by the parties to be legally binding. The law allows for this.

If Tom makes an arrangement to meet Jack at the GPO, in O'Connell Street, on Monday at 8.00 p.m. and Jack fails to turn up, the law will do nothing in this matter. The agreement was not intended to create legal rights and duties and, as such, is not a contract in law. Every contract is an agreement but not every agreement is a contract.

The aim of the law of contract is to identify those agreements which it will enforce and those agreements which it will not. All valid contracts must contain essential elements, for example, Offer and Acceptance. There must be an agreement between the parties to a contract: one party must have made an offer and the other party must have accepted it. The person making the offer is called the offeror and the person who receives the offer is called the offeree. The contract comes into existence when an offer has been unconditionally accepted. The offer may be made orally, in writing or by conduct and the offer may be made to a definite person or to the whole world. An offer ceases to exist in the following circumstances:

(1) on the death of either the offeror or the offeree before acceptance;
(2) by non-acceptance within the time stipulated or laid down for acceptance;
(3) within a reasonable time;
(4) when revoked before acceptance;
(5) when rejected by the offeree.

Another essential is the intention to create legal relations, that is, that both parties must intend that their agreement be legally enforceable.

It must be borne in mind that it is not possible to make an agreement which ousts the jurisdiction of the courts. Access to the courts is open to all persons to test their rights and it is for the courts to decide whether rights do or do not exist or whether a remedy will or will not be granted.

Another essential is consideration. There are a minimum of two parties to a contract and each party has responsibilities. All of the duties and responsibilities must not lie on one party. When a person leaves his lawnmower in to be serviced, he agrees to pay for the jobs that have to be done. This reciprocity is called consideration and unless there is consideration there cannot be a binding, legally valid contract. An interesting feature of consideration is that it need not be adequate.

The general rule of the law of contract is that the parties are free to make what contracts they wish, that is, by naming the price for which they are prepared to sell their goods and the price for which the purchaser is prepared to give. *Caveat emptor* (let the buyer beware) is a very basic rule. If I buy for £1 a picture which turns out to be a masterpiece, e.g. a Rembrandt, I am fortunate whereas the seller is not. The contract, nevertheless, is good and binding.

Other essentials which ought to be borne in mind are the capacity to enter into a valid contract. Both parties must be legally capable of making a contract, that is, where persons are concerned each person must be eighteen years of age or upwards. A party to a valid, binding contract must, in fact, enter into the contract freely; in other words, there must be a genuine and proper consent. If duress, which means violence or threatened violence, is exercised on a party to a contract or if there is undue influence, it will be open to the injured party to ask a court to set the contract aside. It should be remembered that marriage is, in law, a contract and that marriages have been annulled where it was established that a true and proper consent did not exist at the time of contracting the marriage (*see* ANNULMENT).

Finally, the object or the purpose of the contract must not be tainted by illegality. Illegality may be involved in the making of a contract, in the performance of a contract, in the consideration of a contract or, indeed, in the purpose of a contract. A word about each in turn.

Illegality may exist in regard to the making of a contract. For example, a contract which amounts to a criminal conspiracy is, of course, illegal. Illegality may exist in regard to the performance, as in a contract to perform an illegal operation. The consideration itself may be contrary to law as in a contract to live off immoral earnings from prostitution. Finally, illegality may exist in regard to the purpose of a contract as in a contract to lease a room for the purpose of sheltering criminals.

Many of the transactions which occur daily are, in effect, contracts and do not require advice or consideration or thinking about. But should one be contemplating entering into a contract that is difficult, it is advisable in the circumstances to seek legal advice through a solicitor.

Many contracts are carried out according to the terms and clauses which govern them but some, in fact, are not fulfilled. The law provides remedies for breach of contract and these remedies may be in the form of damages for actual loss suffered. Where a party is not able to complete his side of the contract in full he may claim what is called a *quantum meruit,* which means as much as is deserved. It would be wrong if, say, a plumber supplies piping, time and effort and completes 90 per cent of the contract but is not able to complete the remaining 10 per cent. For that plumber not to receive some remuneration would be clearly unjust. Occasionally it is open to a party to seek an injunction where there has been a breach of contract. Finally, it may be open to a person to seek specific performance. Specific performance may be granted by the court where it is shown that a person agreed to sell and then decided after the contract had been concluded not to sell. The court may take the view that such a situation is unjust and inequitable and that it works hardship on the purchaser and may order specific performance which is an order forcing the seller to complete the sale.

CONVEYANCING

Conveyancing may be simply defined as that area of law which deals with the transfer and acquisition of the ownership of land. It has the public perception of being a very simple procedure and an easy money earner for solicitors. While it is true that once the procedures are learned and understood it is not very difficult, each transaction is separate and a very high standard of care must be given to each individual dealing. Just as a doctor removing an appendix is performing a very simple procedure, he must do each one to the highest standard of care or drastic consequences can ensue. Likewise in conveyancing: the object of this chapter is to explain what is involved when houses and pieces of land are bought and sold. It is proposed to deal with it under a number of headings, the first of which is the contract.

Contract

The sale and purchase of land and houses are governed by Section 2 of the Statute of Frauds (Ireland) Act, 1695. The general rule is that all contracts for the sale of land must be in writing. However, this definition is not strictly true as what the Act requires is that any agreement to sell land be evidenced in writing. So, in some circumstances, an oral agreement to sell land can be enforceable provided the existence of the oral agreement can be evidenced in writing. This is a very complex area of the law and there is a great amount of case law as to what would constitute sufficient evidence of such an oral agreement. It is necessary, at the very minimum, that such written evidence can establish the parties to the transaction, the purchase price and a full description of the property. However, in most cases, the contract is reduced to writing in the form of the Law Society's standard form of particulars and conditions of sale. This contract deals with the following matters:

(a) Makes provision for a consent of a spouse who must agree to the sale of a property by another spouse. It is a provision of the Family Home Protection Act, 1976 that a spouse cannot sell any property which is a family home without the consent of the other spouse. This must be a prior consent and accordingly must be endorsed on the contract prior to its being signed by the spouse who is the owner of the property.

(b)　Makes provision for the names and addresses of the parties to the transaction.

(c)　It sets out the purchase price and the deposit.

(d)　There is provision made for the insertion of the closing date. This is the date on which the parties to the contract agree the deal should be finalised, the purchase money paid over and the deeds and keys to the property handed across. If the transaction is not finalised on the closing date the purchaser who is in default is liable to pay interest to the vendor on the balance of the purchase money still outstanding at a penal rate of interest which is set out in the contract. When a purchaser is in such default it is normal for the vendor or his solicitor to serve a notice on the purchaser requiring him to complete the transaction within twenty-eight days. If the transaction is then not completed within that time the vendor may forfeit any deposit paid by the purchaser, he may then resell the property and if he suffers a loss as a result of this resale, he is entitled to sue the original purchaser for such loss. A further remedy available to both the vendor and purchaser in a situation where the other party is refusing to complete is to go to court to get an order of the Court specifically performing the contract.

(e)　Interest Rate. The interest rate as mentioned above is normally a penal one which is inserted in the contract to ensure that the purchaser takes the transaction seriously and will always find it more prudent to close on time than not. This rate is one of the reasons why people go on bridging finance: it is cheaper to pay a bank's interest rate than to pay a penal rate to the vendor. A purchaser in this situation must obtain the vendor's tax number and should deduct 27 per cent (the current rate) from it and send it on to the vendor's Inspector of Taxes.

(f)　The contract will also make provision whereby the vendor's solicitor will acknowledge that he holds the deposit as a stakeholder. It is normal in most conveyancing transactions for the deposit to be held as stakeholder between the parties and not to be released to the vendor or returned to the purchaser until the transaction has been finalised.

(g)　The contract also sets out the particulars and tenure of the property. This means a full description of the property

inserted by which the property can be fully identified. Sometimes a map is annexed to the contract to clarify the description. It will also set out the tenure. Tenure indicates how land is held. In general in this country, land is either freehold or leasehold.

A freehold interest in property is the highest interest that can be held by an individual and in general such an owner is free to do with the land as he wishes. However, in recent times, various legislative enactments have encroached upon this freedom. Generally the mines and minerals in land are vested in the state and also acts such as the Compulsory Purchase Acts and the Planning Acts place serious curtailments on the freeholder. There are other freehold estates which are not of common use and which we will not deal with in this present book.

A leasehold interest is less than a freehold interest in that it is for a term of years and accordingly will end at some date in the future. It creates the relationship of landlord and tenant and is governed by the provisions of Deasy's Act, 1860. Section 3 of Deasy's Act establishes that the relationship of landlord and tenant is founded on contract. The contract has to set out the full details of the lease, that is, the parties, the term, the rent.

(h) The contract will also list the various documents which have to be shown prior to the contract being signed. A purchaser who signs a contract without inspecting all the documents which are made available to him is deemed to have full notice of them and is caught by the consequences of any onerous conditions which may appear in them. An example of this would be a restrictive covenant restricting a purchaser's use of the property in some way or other. It is not unusual for a planning authority to sterilise land on the granting of planning permission for the erection of a house so that no other houses can be erected on that piece of land. The Document Schedule normally contains copies of the various documents of title and may also contain copies of any planning permission.

(i) The contract also makes provision for whatever searches are to be made available by the vendor to the purchaser. We will explain in greater detail what this means in due course (*see* page 42).

The contract then continues with a number of standard conditions. The most significant of these contains the procedure to be followed when a property is bought and sold at auction, a number of warranties and in particular a warranty that any development of the land since 1 October 1964 has full and proper planning permission.

Registration

In Ireland there are two types of title. These are what are known as registered title and unregistered title. Registered title is one that is guaranteed by the state and is registered in the Land Registry. Registered land was first introduced by the local Registration of Title (Ireland) Act, 1891. Once a title is registered a register is maintained in the Land Registry. In general there are three parts to a register. Part one will set out the description of the property by reference to a map which is also retained in the Land Registry. Part two sets out the ownership to the property. Part three sets out any burdens to which the property is subject. The most common burden affecting most people's property is a mortgage. This register or folio is, in the absence of fraud, conclusive evidence of a person's ownership. Accordingly, when one wishes to sell property one merely has to show a copy of the folio, i.e. a copy of the Register, with the contract, to establish one's right to sell. On the transfer of ownership a Deed of Transfer is lodged in the Land Registry; on receipt of this the Registrar will delete the registered owner's name and substitute that of the new owner. This is very similar to a transfer of shares in a limited company.

The system in relation to unregistered land is totally different. In this system title to property is deduced from reading the title documents. It will be seen that in this method it is necessary to retain all the title documents together, as on each sale one has to establish title and furnish copies of them. There are, however, restrictions on the amount of title one has to show. One invariably finds that all the title documents are kept in a bundle. These deeds are registered in the Registry of Deeds. The particulars of the date of registration, the actual time of registration, the book and reference number are endorsed on the deed. This system of registration was established by the Registration of Deeds Act, 1707. A memorial of a deed, which is in essence a precis form of the deed, is lodged in the Registry of Deeds and retained there. The registration particulars are endorsed on the deed. The principal reason for registering deeds in the Registry of Deeds is that it governs priorities and conflicts between deeds. For example, if two mortgages on the one piece of property are taken out with two lending institutions on the same day, the lending institution which registers its mortgage first will have priority over the other.

Searches

Searches are basically enquiries that a purchaser should make in the course of purchasing property. There are some which should be made prior to the contract being executed and some which are made on the date of closing the transaction. The pre-contractual searches are as follows:

(a) *Planning Search.* A planning search should be made in the Planning Office. This will disclose three basic things to a purchaser. It will let him know how the property is zoned, be it residential, commercial or otherwise; whether there are any proposals for road widening in the area; and whether or not any applications for planning permission in respect of the property have been granted—or indeed refused. This could be of great importance to a purchaser who is purchasing the property with the intention of making some commercial use of it. If he were to discover that a planning application for a similar purpose had been turned down in the past he would be very imprudent to proceed with the transaction. When someone is purchasing property and discovers that since 1 October 1964 there has been a development on the property, or an alteration or change of user and that if this is not shown in the Planning Office he will know that the vendor has not obtained proper planning permission. Enquiries will then have to be made of the vendor. Sometimes it will be necessary to obtain a retention order, that is permission to retain an unauthorised structure. This can actually take a long time and may ultimately be refused.

(b) *A Licensing Search.* This takes place when a purchaser is buying a pub or hotel. A licensing search should be made to establish the nature of the licence, for example, a seven day on licence, a hotel licence, etc., and the extent to which the premises are licensed. It should also show whether or not there are any convictions on the licence.

(c) **A Compulsory Purchase Order Search.** This is self-explanatory and should be made with the local authority to establish whether or not any plans are afoot to acquire the property compulsorily or indeed if any notices have been served. If a Compulsory Purchase Order has been made it is not possible for the vendor to give good title as the property no longer, strictly speaking, vests in him and he will accordingly be unable to vest it in somebody else. An example where a Compulsory Purchase Order is often used is to acquire land for the purpose of road widening.

The following searches are done on the day of closing:

(a) **A Land Registry Search.** This, as already indicated, is a search in the Land Registry to inspect the register or folio to find what the up-to-date position is. Such a search will establish the ownership of the property, the title whether absolute or possessory, whether it is leasehold or freehold, whether or not there are mortgages, rights of residence or other restrictions on the folio. One should mention in relation to registered land that there are some burdens which take effect without registration and these are set out in Section 72 of the Registration of Title Act, 1964, for example, outstanding estate duty, succession duty, rent charges, land improvement charges, annuities, rights of the public, tenancies created for a term not exceeding twenty-one years and so on. It is normal conveyancing procedure for a vendor to swear an affidavit to the effect that none of these burdens affects the property. A purchaser on receipt of such an affidavit would be deemed to be taking the property bona fide without notice of any such burden.

(b) **A Company Search.** This is a search made in the Companies Registration Office which will confirm that the company exists and is still on the register and also will disclose any charges which exist against it. It will also disclose the existence of a winding-up order or petition. It is normal on closing to get a certificate from the Company Secretary certifying that no resolution has been passed to wind up the company.

(c) **A Judgment Search.** This is done in the Central Office of the High Court and will disclose basically two things: any lis pendens affecting the property and any monetary judgments against the vendor. A *lis pendens* is a record of the existence of litigation affecting the property. The purchaser, once he is aware of this, and if he proceeded to close the deal, would take the property subject to the consequences of the outcome of that particular litigation. The judgment search will also disclose any monetary debts owed by the vendor. These do not affect the property being sold but merely put the purchaser on notice of the possibility of such a debt having been converted into a type of mortgage known as a judgment mortgage. A judgment mortgage is a judgment for money against a party which has been converted into a mortgage and registered against the property.

(d) *Bankruptcy Search.* This is self-evident and will disclose whether or not the vendor is bankrupt. If a person is bankrupt his property will vest in the Official Assignee, that is the court official in charge of bankruptcy, and such a person could not transfer good title.

(e) *Sheriff and Revenue Sheriff Searches.* These are only done in the case of leasehold property as a sheriff only has power to seize personal goods and leasehold property is defined as personalty. Such a search will disclose any warrants lodged with the sheriff for the recovery of money against a vendor. A purchaser who is aware of the existence of such a warrant takes due notice of it and is subject to it. Prior to closing such a transaction a purchaser will insist that the vendor discharges the particular debt and obtains confirmation from the creditor that the debt is no longer due.

(f) *Registry of Deeds Searches.* As the name indicates this search is carried out on an index of names in the Registry of Deeds to establish whether or not any deeds or judgment mortgages have been registered affecting the property. Such a search is made against a person from the date on which the deed to him was dated until such date as a deed from him to a purchaser is registered.

Who can Sell?

We will now set out the various people and the capacity in which they can sell and transfer land.

(a) The most obvious person is of course the owner of the property. This person has a clear right to sell the property subject to the restriction mentioned above imposed by the provisions of the Family Home Protection Act, 1976. Any transfer of property which infringes this act and is carried out without the consent of the appropriate spouse is void and of no effect.

(b) A legal personal representative of a deceased person. You will note from the chapter dealing with death that the legal personal representative is normally the executor in a testate case and the next-of-kin in an intestate case. Such a person has a power to sell the property but he must always remember that he stands in the position of a trustee *vis-à-vis* the beneficiaries. This means he must take steps to ensure that he gets a proper price for the property. He does not absolutely have to ensure that he gets the best price available in the entire world but he must obtain the market value. If he does not he would of course be in breach of trust and he would be personally liable for any shortfall.

(c) A tenant for life under the Settled Land Acts has power of sale which was given to him by virtue of Section 3 of the Settled Land Act, 1882. A tenant for life is a person who has a life interest in the property and on his death the property will become the property of some other person known as the remainder man. When a tenant for life sells the property he must invest the capital and preserve it so that on his death the capital is available to go to the remainder man. In the meantime he is entitled to take the interest of the capital. A tenant for life also has power to grant leases and to mortgage the property.

(d) The trustees of the settlement with power of sale may of course sell land. Once again they are under a fiduciary duty to the beneficiaries and must act at all times in their best interest and may not break the settlement.

(e) A mortgagee in possession. When an owner of property defaults on his mortgage the mortgage deed gives a power to the mortgage company to repossess the property and to sell it so as to realise the debt. Such a mortgagee must act correctly and may not sell the property at an under value just to realise his own debt. When such a mortgagee sells property he will of course satisfy his own debt and costs and then should pay over to the owner any balance left over.

(f) Official assignee in bankruptcy. When a person is declared a bankrupt all his estate vests in the official assignee and as a consequence of this the official assignee can sell the property and give good title to a purchaser.

(g) Liquidator of a company. When a company goes into liquidation and a liquidator is validly appointed such a liquidator has a power of sale to realise all the assets of the company including land. Such a liquidator would be under a duty to obtain a proper price for the property and may only use the proceeds to discharge creditors in the correct order.

(h) Receiver. A receiver properly appointed under a power in a debenture may also exercise a right of sale.

What Documents are used to Convey Property?

(a) In relation to registered land, be it freehold or leasehold, the document to be used is a Deed of Transfer, the format of which is prescribed by the Land Registry Rules, 1972.

(b) A Deed of Conveyance is used to transfer freehold unregistered land.

(c) A Deed of Assignment is used to transfer leasehold unregistered land.

(d) A Deed of Mortgage is used to transfer the title to the property to the mortgagee for the duration of the mortgage. If the mortgagor, that is the person getting the mortgage, is a limited company a form 47 setting out details of the mortgage must be filed in the Companies Office within twenty-one days of the date of the mortgage. If this is not done such a mortgage may lose its priority and it will also be necessary to obtain a court order getting liberty to file such a form out of time. Most mortgages are in a format that can be used for unregistered or registered land. In relation to registered land they include a charging clause which effectively charges the land and is registered as a burden on Part III of the Register or Folio.

(e) A Vacate. A Vacate is an official receipt by a bank or building society or local authority acknowledging that a mortgage has been paid off and effecting the retransfer of the title from the mortgagee to the mortgagor.

At this point, it is necessary to say a few words about Deeds of Transfer, Conveyance and Assignment. These can be for full value or they can be for partial value or can be voluntary. If they are for full value they will have to be signed by both parties, be properly stamped and must also bear the particulars delivered stamp. The particulars delivered stamp indicates that a form has been given to the Revenue setting out details of the transaction. They will also have to contain certain certificates for the Revenue such as a transaction certificate and a certificate pursuant to Section 112 of the Finance Act, 1990. They would also contain certificates pursuant to the Land Act certifying that the property being purchased is being bought by an Irish citizen or that the property is situated in an urban area. (Such consents are only required for non-urban land.) In the event that the purchaser is not an Irish citizen it must be certified that the appropriate consent of the Land Commission has been obtained. Consents which used to be issued by the now defunct Land Commission will in future come under the auspices of the Department of Lands. Note also that if the consideration, that is the purchase money, exceeds £100,000 it is necessary to obtain a certificate of clearance from Capital Gains Tax. If this is not forthcoming the purchaser is obligated to stop a proportion of the purchase price which he must send to the Revenue Commissioners from whom the vendor will, in due course, have to obtain a refund of this money, and if the price exceeds £91,000 a certificate of clearance from Residential Property Tax is required. If any of these transactions are either voluntary or below full value a number of consequences arise. They are:

(a) A Certificate of Clearance from Capital Acquisition Tax must be obtained.

(b) A Declaration of Solvency by the donor to the effect that he was solvent and able to pay his debts without recourse to the property in the transaction prior to the execution of the particular deed.

(c) Such a donor should declare that he was independently advised or that he was offered independent advice and also that it was his express wish that the particular deed should be irrevocable. In a situation where such a donor did not have independent legal advice it is very prudent of a purchaser to insist that an insurance bond be made available to cover the possibility of such a deed being revoked. The presumption that arises in these cases is that such a conveyance was brought about by undue influence by the donee over the donor. In this situation it will be necessary to obtain a Certificate of Discharge from Capital Acquisition Tax. This certificate shows that the Revenue Commissioners are satisfied with the tax situation.

Other Means of Transfer

The transfer of property may also be effected by a transfer of shares in a company. This arises where company X owns property. Company X has four shareholders. Company X puts the land in the hands of an auctioneer who eventually introduces a purchaser. The purchaser may buy the property by way of a purchase of shares in Company X.

A transfer effected in this way has some advantages and some disadvantages. The major advantage is the saving of stamp duty. If we take a hypothetical situation where the property being sold is valued at £100,000, the stamp duty paid by a purchaser on such a transaction is £6,000, being 6 per cent of the purchase money. However, if the transfer is effected by a transfer of shares in a company the stamp duty is £1,000 because the stamp duty on a transfer of shares only attracts a rate of 1 per cent. The main disadvantages of such a transfer is of course that the new purchasers who effectively become the company take the company warts and all; so the purchaser would need to have the company's books audited and get absolute indemnities that all tax and debts due by the company are in order.

This method of transaction also has a significant disadvantage for capital gains purposes. A capital gain arises when somebody purchases an item for x pounds and then subsequently sells it for x + y pounds. The gain in question is y pounds. In the situation we have set out above there is no change of ownership in the property and accordingly any subsequent sale by the company under the control of its new shareholders will have to use the cost for which X company originally bought the property as its base valuation for calculating the capital gains situation. If the company has held the property for a long time this could have very serious consequences.

Your Average House

The following are the normal steps to be taken in the purchase of an average house.

(a) A person buying a house must first of all understand the total financial consequences of such a purchase. These will obviously involve the price of the house. However, there are many hidden items of which he should be aware. Apart from the purchase price the following list of expenses will arise:

(i) *Stamp duty.* The rates of stamp duty are as follows: from £0 to £5,000, 0 per cent; from £5,000 to £10,000, 1 per cent; from £10,000 to £15,000, 2 per cent; from £15,000 to £25,000, 3 per cent; from £25,000 to £50,000, 4 per cent; from £50,000 to £60,000, 5 per cent and from

£60,000 upwards, 6 per cent. Stamp duty is also payable on the mortgage which is at the rate of £1 per thousand. Most mortgages incorporate a requirement that the mortgagors effect life assurance, i.e. mortgage protection, so as to protect the mortgage. There is an assignment of this policy to the building society or bank and this attracts a stamp duty rate of £10.

(ii) *Search fees.* These, as already indicated, are enquiries which have to be made by the purchaser and carried out by professional firms of searchers. The average cost is in the range of about £65 to £85. They can of course be greater or lesser depending on the extent of the enquiries to be made.

(iii) *Solicitor's fees.* These are normally 1 per cent plus £100 plus 21 per cent VAT.

(iv) *Surveyor's fees.* These vary a bit but are generally in the range of £100 plus VAT. This is money very well spent and it is a very foolish purchaser who buys a house without having a proper survey carried out.

(v) The building society will normally have an *acceptance fee* and also their solicitor may have a *small handling fee.*

(vi) *Registration fee.* When a person purchases a house his title deeds have to be registered either in the Land Registry or in the Registry of Deeds. The average fee in the Land Registry is £250 while the Registry of Deeds is normally £52, that is £26 for the purchase deed and £26 for the mortgage.

(vii) *Insurance.* It is essential that adequate structure insurance be placed on a premises in the event of it being destroyed by fire. Insurance cover should be sufficient to enable the building to be reinstated. Underinsurance in this situation can have drastic consequences (*see* page 112). Once a person signs a contract he has an equitable interest in the property and can in fact insure the property as and from that date. However, the current standard form of contract for sale provides that the vendor should insure the property up until the closing date and thereafter the purchaser should insure it. If the purchaser is obtaining a mortgage his building society or bank will also ensure that their interest is noted on the insurance policy.

(b) Having chosen a house the purchaser should do two things:

(*i*) He must get a proper survey carried out on the house. It is quite likely that his bank or his building society will insist on this. It must be realised that the bank or building society survey the house basically from their own point of view, that is their ability to realise the asset in the event of default. However, a purchaser will have to live in the house and put up with rising damp, creaking floor boards and other defects. This should be carried out before the contract is signed.

(*ii*) The purchaser should instruct his solicitor giving him full details of the transaction. He should draw his attention to any unusual features about the house and in particular should draw his attention to any extensions or alterations to the property or anything that might need planning permission. If the property is served by a septic tank this should also be brought to the attention of the solicitor so that he can clarify the matter and ensure that the septic tank is either within the site or if off the site that proper wayleave is available.

When an agreement for a sale has been reached the auctioneer or the vendor will instruct the vendor's solicitor whose duty it is to prepare the contract and send out sufficient title to the purchaser's solicitor. On receipt of the title the purchaser's solicitor will of course investigate the title. Having done this he will then invite his client in to sign the contract. The solicitor will at this point in time explain any unusual features of the title to the purchaser before the contract is signed. If the purchaser is happy he will then sign the contract and put his solicitor in funds for the deposit which is usually 10 per cent of the purchase price. If the purchaser is obtaining a loan the contract will of course be made subject to the purchaser obtaining the loan and also being able to comply with all the conditions contained in such loan approval.

The purchaser's solicitor now drafts the purchase deed and raises his objections and requisitions on title. Objections and requisitions on title are a series of queries in relation to the title made by the purchaser. The purchaser's solicitor then sends off the contract together with the deposit, the draft deed and these objections and requisitions for the vendor's solicitor's attention. By now, the purchaser has committed himself to a sale subject to any condition he may have inserted in the contract—for example, subject to loan clause. The vendor, however, is not usually committed to the sale until he signs the contract and returns it to a purchaser. This puts the purchaser at a disadvantage: he has to commit himself first to the transaction.

If the vendor is proceeding with the sale he now signs the contract and his solicitor returns one part of it to the purchaser's solicitor. The vendor's solicitor also approves the draft deed and returns it duly approved for engrossment by the purchaser's solicitor. He also returns one part of the objections and requisitions on title answered. On receipt of these documents the purchaser's solicitor checks the replies to the objections and requisitions and if they are in order he confirms this to the vendor's solicitor. If they are not in order he issues rejoinders. He now engrosses, that is types up, the purchase deed and returns it to the vendor's solicitor for execution, that is signing by the vendor. By this time the purchaser will usually have obtained his loan approval.

Some banks and building societies issue the loan cheque direct to the purchaser's solicitor on foot of his undertaking to carry out the registration of the title and execution of the mortgage and to hold the purchase deeds in trust for the building society or bank pending completion of these matters. Other banks and building societies instruct their own solicitor and in this situation the purchaser's solicitor would have to communicate with the building society solicitor. When the purchaser's solicitor has completed this portion of the transaction he checks with the lending institution to confirm that the loan cheque is available and ready to issue. On the assumption that it is, he then sets up an appointment to close the transaction. The purchaser's solicitor now requisitions his Land Registry or Registry of Deeds, Companies Office, Judgment, Bankruptcy and Sheriff searches as the case may be. The purchaser puts a solicitor in funds for the balance of the purchase money and also for the stamp duty and registration fees. At the closing the vendor's solicitor hands over to the purchaser's solicitor all the title documents, the documentation arising out of the requisitions on title, receipts for outgoings, keys and the purchase deed duly executed by the vendor. In exchange he is paid the balance of the purchase money. This is the moment when the ownership changes and the transaction is concluded as far as the vendor is concerned.

The purchaser's solicitor will now have to attend to the stamping and registration of the document; in some cases this may be taken over by a solicitor acting for the building society.

The documents must be stamped within twenty-eight days of execution to avoid attracting extremely high penalties. When the deeds have been registered in the ordinary situation they are lodged with the bank or building society and retained there until such time as the mortgage is redeemed.

We now propose listing a number of items which turn up in conveyancing which must be understood by a purchaser.

(a) **Ownership.** When two or more people are buying property together they are deemed to be co-owners. There are two principal types of co-ownership in existence, joint tenancy and a tenancy in common. In a joint tenancy all the people own the property as one legal entity. On the death of one co-owner in a joint tenancy his interest accrues to the remaining co-owners. This is known as the jus accrescendi, that is the right of survivorship. This form of ownership is used principally where married couples buy property so that on the death of one the ownership of the property automatically accrues to the other. In a tenancy in common the various co-owners are deemed to own an undivided share of the property. This means that if one co-owner in a tenancy in common dies his interest in the property does not accrue to the remaining co-owners but rather devolves to his estate. In short, he can dispose of his share by Will. This type of co-ownership is clearly more suited for business and commercial transactions.

(b) **Easements.** An easement is the right of an owner of property in the land of another owner. Examples of an easement are right-of-way, right to light, right to support etc. These are acquired in a number of ways: principally by express grant or reservation; by implied grant or reservation; and by prescription.

(c) **Fixtures and Fittings.** Fixtures which attached to the land are normally included in all sales unless they are specifically excluded. These matters should be ironed out in the pre-contractual stage. In the event of any doubt the contract should set out what is included and what is excluded. What is a fixture and what is not a fixture has been the subject of many law cases. The degree of annexation and the purpose of annexation are decisive. The purpose of annexation is the determining feature in this regard. For example, looms in the sale of a mill were held by the courts to be fixtures while

tapestry attached to a wall in the sale of a mansion was not. Fittings are normally not included in the sale unless expressly provided for. Therefore it is very advisable when the sale is being agreed that all these matters be ironed out.

Family Home Protection Act, 1976

As already indicated above, this Act curtails the right of an owner to sell the family home without the prior consent of his or her spouse. A family home is defined in Section 2 of the Act as a dwelling in which a married couple ordinarily reside. The expression comprises, in addition, a dwelling in which a spouse whose protection is in issue ordinarily resides or—if that spouse has left the other spouse—ordinarily resided before so leaving. A dwelling is any building, structure, vehicle or vessel (or part thereof) occupied as a separate unit. It includes any garden or portion of ground attached to it. Any transfer of property in contravention of this particular act is void and of no effect.

The Family Law Act, 1981

This Act deals with the position of engaged couples. The Act is unusual in that Section 2 states that an agreement to marry is not enforceable at law and then proceeds to set out a number of consequences of an engagement. Section 2 sets out that where a wedding gift is given to a couple who are engaged to be married it is deemed to be given to them as joint tenants. Section 4 states that, where a party to an agreement to marry makes a gift to the other party, it shall be returned to the donor should the marriage not take place for any reason other than the death of the donor. If conveyancing is concerned it may be necessary to get the recipient to release any interest he or she has in a property which is in the ownership of the other.

The Judicial Separation and Law Reform Act, 1989

This is a long and quite complicated Act. However, in relation to conveyancing, it is necessary to get an affidavit to confirm that any transfer of property is not for the purposes of defeating the claim for financial relief within the meaning of Section 29 of this Act. The declaration should also confirm that the person selling the property acquired it after 18 October 1989 without notice of any intention to defeat a claim for financial relief.

Apartment Blocks

These have become a common feature of Ireland in the last

twenty years. They are normally run by a management company. The management company is set up originally by the developer. It is generally a company limited by guarantee and the number of shares in the company is normally equal to the number of apartments in the complex. As each apartment is sold off each purchaser becomes a member of the company and thus a shareholder. When the entire complex is sold all the shares in the management company will now be owned by all the new owners of the apartments. This effectively means that the owners of the various apartments are now the management company and must look after the running of the complex. The management company will attend to a number of things, the principal of which are to effect block insurance on the complex and to attend to on-going repairs. It should also create a sinking fund where money is put aside for a rainy day in the event of some major structural damage to the complex. The management company generally elects a committee to run the management of the complex and set the service charge. The service charge is an annual fee payable by all the members to cover the costs and outlays incurred by the management company. It is very much in the interests of the owners of apartments to ensure that this company functions correctly. Occasionally these companies break down and it is almost impossible for anyone to get insurance for their own individual apartment. It also creates major problems in relation to maintenance of common areas. On the sale of any apartment the vendor will hand over a share transfer form which effectively transfers his membership of the management company to the new purchaser who will then become a member.

Sub-division

In relation to rural land, if a person is transferring part of his holding it is necessary to obtain the consent of the Department of Lands to sub-divide. If the consent is granted it is often subject to conditions which have to be complied with before the consent is deemed to be full and proper. One of the more common such conditions is that the land purchase annuity on the property be redeemed. It may also be a condition that an unregistered holding be registered or that the holding being purchased by the new owner be consolidated with some existing holding he already owns. The philosophy behind this legislation was to prevent the creation of uneconomic agricultural holdings. There is, however, an exception to this in relation to a small plot of land of less than one acre. In this situation formal consent is not needed.

Commercial Leases

These are leases for a term of years and they create the relationship of landlord and tenant between the parties. The most important clauses are of course the rent review clause and the user clause. The rent review normally sets up a mechanism whereby the rent is reviewed every so often. The user clause sets out the permitted use that a lessee may make of the particular property. This clause is effectively the landlord's way of controlling the use made of various units in a complex. The lease will also make provision for service charges. These normally deal with block insurance, security and maintenance and upkeep of common areas. The creation of some commercial leases can also give rise to VAT and if a lessee is not registered for VAT this can have dire consequences for him. The VAT normally payable is equal roughly to one year's rent. If the lessee is not registered for VAT he has no way of claiming this back and accordingly will have to fund it out of his own resources.

Short-term Leases of Flats

This is about bedsitters. The leases may be in writing or they may arise implicitly once rent is paid on a week-to-week basis or a month-to-month basis. They can be terminated by either party on giving the appropriate notice. This notice may be set out in the written document. If it is not then the notice will be one week in respect of a weekly tenancy and one month in respect of a monthly tenancy. It is usually necessary for a landlord to obtain a court order to eject a tenant in this situation. The first procedure is to serve a Notice to Quit terminating the tenancy. A landlord will normally have to go to court to get a court order giving possession. However, it should be noted that once a tenancy has been terminated, if the landlord can get peaceful possession, that is without breaking into the premises, he is entitled to do so.

In this area the government recently introduced the Housing (Rent Books) Regulations, 1993. Landlords (including housing authorities) are required to provide new tenants on or after 1 September 1993 with rent books at the commencement of the tenancy and to provide existing tenants with rent books not later than 1 November 1993. The rent book must also include specified particulars relating to the tenancy, a statement of the tenant's basic statutory rights and, in the case of a new tenancy, the date of commencement of the tenancy and an inventory of furnishings and appliances supplied by the landlord for the tenant's exclusive use.

The Regulations do not apply to holiday lettings or to formerly rent-controlled dwellings—the latter tenants are already legally entitled to rent books.

Effective from 1 January 1994 for private rented dwellings and 1 January 1998 for dwellings let by housing authorities are the Housing (Standards for Rented Houses) Regulations, 1993. These Regulations oblige the landlords of such dwellings to ensure that they comply with certain minimum standards. The standards relate to
– structural condition
– provision of sinks, toilets, baths/showers, cooking and food storage facilities
– safety of electricity and gas installations
– availability of adequate heating, lighting and ventilation
– maintenance of common areas.

The Regulations do not apply to temporary or holiday lettings and to certain types of accommodation let by health boards and certain approved non-profit or voluntary bodies.

Any person who contravenes a provision of the Regulations is liable to a maximum fine of £1,000 plus a fine of £100 for every day of a continuing offence.

Licences

A licence is a permission to do something in relation to land which would be unlawful if one did not have that permission. There are many and varied types of licences. For example, a bare licence is a permission to do something, e.g. to hunt. Such a licence implies no interest on the licensee and is revocable at the whim of the licensor. However, case law does suggest that a packing-up period be allowed.

Another form of licence is a licence coupled with an interest. This licence does in fact give an interest in the land and a common example of it would be a right to turbary or a right to shoot or fishing rights.

COSTS

Costs, which are the fees and outlays of lawyers, are generally awarded by a court to the victorious side. In this situation the loser will have to pay his own costs and also the costs of the victor. Costs generally are made up of what are called solicitor and client costs and party and party costs. There is a notion abroad that if one loses one's case, one does not have to pay. However, this is not so. If one engages a solicitor to process an action on one's behalf, one would have to pay a fee irrespective of the result. After all, one has to pay a doctor, irrespective of whether or not he cures you. A solicitor's costs in relation to an action are made up of his own fee, the fees he has to pay to barristers engaged on a client's behalf and the costs of professional witnesses. These would include engineers, actuaries and medical witnesses. Further outlay will be involved in relation to issuing the various summonses in the courts and filing/serving various motions and obtaining High Court orders.

Party and party costs are the costs a victorious party recovers against the losing party. These may not be enough to discharge the entire bill of the victorious party, which will include the solicitor's bill to his client. In the situation the party will be expected to make up any shortfall there is between the amount due under the solicitor and client account and the party and party account.

THE COURT SYSTEM
Criminal Courts

Children's Court
In this court a district judge tries cases involving minor crimes committed by children under sixteen years of age. There is no jury and the cases are heard in camera.

District Court
The District Court tries minor offences for which the maximum penalty is twelve months' imprisonment and/or a £1,000 fine. Minor offences include certain road traffic offences e.g. driving without insurance, petty theft, certain forms of assault.

In the case of serious offences such as murder, rape, etc. the District Court carries out a *preliminary investigation* to establish that there is a case to answer. The District judge examines the evidence presented by the prosecution and the defence. If there is sufficient evidence, the judge will return the defendant for trial to a higher court e.g. Circuit Court, Central Criminal Court, etc. Where the District judge is not satisfied that there is a case, the defendant is discharged.

Circuit Court
This court consists of a judge and jury. It hears serious offences

such as assaults, robbery, etc. It also hears appeals from those convicted in the District Court.

Central Criminal Court
This court tries very serious offences such as treason, murder, attempted murder, conspiracy to murder, rape, serious sexual assaults, piracy and certain offences under the Treason Act, 1939 and the Offences Against the State Act, 1939. It also hears appeals from the Circuit Court. It consists of a judge and jury.

Court of Criminal Appeal
This court consists of not less than three judges. It hears appeals from the Circuit Court, the Central Criminal Court and the Special Criminal Court. The appeal is not a rehearing of the case but is based on the transcript of the evidence given at the original trial.

Special Criminal Court
Article 38.3 of the constitution provides that special courts may be established for the trial of offences in cases where it is determined that the ordinary courts are inadequate to secure the effective administration of justice and the preservation of public peace and order. It deals with cases relating to the Offences Against the State Act, which are generally, though not always, of a subversive nature.

The Special Criminal Court consists of at least three judges. There is no jury. At present, there is one such court and it sits in Dublin.

Supreme Court
This court hears appeals from other courts often involving points of law of exceptional public importance. Appeals relating to the granting or refusing of habeas corpus and other orders may also be taken to this court. It consists of at least three judges.

Civil System
District Court
The District Court deals with issues relating to contracts and to civil wrongs where an award of damages may be up to £5,000. Other matters within its jurisdiction include the granting of barring and protection orders, the granting of pub licences, landlord and tenant matters such as ejectment for non-payment of rent, maintenance to deserted wives (£100 limit), etc. There is a judge but no jury.

Circuit Court

This court deals with issues relating to contracts and to civil wrongs where the award of damages may be up to £30,000. Other matters within its jurisdiction include the granting of new club licences; matrimonial cases, e.g. separation, custody, maintenance to deserted wives (unlimited); execution of trusts. It may also hear appeals from the District Court and the Employment Appeals Tribunal.

High Court

The High Court can award unlimited damages in contract and personal injuries cases. Its jurisdiction is very wide and includes succession matters; injunctions; defamation; habeas corpus matters; matrimonial proceedings such as annulment, judicial separations, custody. Its opinion on a point of law may be requested by parties to a case in the District Court. It also hears appeals.

Supreme Court

The Supreme Court is mainly a court of appeal. It hears appeals from the High Court. If the case before it relates to a constitutional issue, then the court consists of five judges; if not, it sits with three judges. It is also a consultative court. The President may refer Bills to the court for a decision as to their constitutionality. In addition, the Circuit Court and High Court may seek its opinion on points of law that have arisen in cases before them.

Court of Justice (An EC court sitting in Luxembourg)

The main functions of the Court of Justice are to ensure that European Community law is enforced, to resolve disputes between member states and the EC and to protect individual rights granted by the various treaties. It is composed of thirteen judges, one from each member state, with one additional judge appointed for staggered terms of six years.

The court is assisted by six *advocates-general* who present opinions on the cases before the court and recommendations for a decision. They are qualified in the same way as the judges.

To ease the workload of the Court of Justice, which was becoming untenable, the Single European Act provided for the creation of a new court, the *Court of First Instance.* It began sitting in 1989. Its jurisdiction is limited to EC staff cases, i.e. disputes between the EC institutions and its staff, competition cases and certain matters relating to the European Coal and Steel Community and Euratom. Its decisions may be appealed to the Court of Justice.

European Court of Human Rights (Strasbourg)
Under the convention of Human Rights, to which Ireland is a signatory, an injured party may petition the European Commission of Human Rights where a state has in some way violated rights set out in the convention. If the Commission is unsuccessful in resolving the matter, the case goes to the Court of Human Rights. One example is the *Airey* v. *Ireland* case, where Ireland was held to have been in breach of the convention because of its failure to provide legal aid in matrimonial cases. The *Norris* case is another example.

Decisions of the court do not bind Irish courts; pressure to comply comes from the political forum as, being signatories to the convention, there are obvious obligations to honour it.

CRIME

Criminal law is concerned with conduct which the state considers should be punished. For the proper functioning and well-being of any society, certain rules are introduced establishing standards of behaviour which that society requires to be observed. Failure to meet these standards is not only an offence against a victim (if there is one) but is also an offence against society. The fact that it is society which is offended explains why in a criminal trial it is the state that prosecutes rather than the victim and the victim is viewed as a witness in the whole process.

When the state successfully prosecutes a wrongdoer and secures a conviction, a penalty is imposed. The purpose of the penalty is obviously primarily to punish the wrongdoer; however, deterring others from engaging in such behaviour and also possible reform of the wrongdoer are considerations. Penalties include: probation, community service orders, fines and imprisonment. The death penalty was abolished in the Criminal Justice Act, 1990.

Fines

These vary depending on the nature of the offence and what various Acts dictate for particular situations. The fines are generally paid to the State and go to the Exchequer. Usually fines are imposed for relatively minor crimes, e.g. parking offences.

Imprisonment

A person found guilty of a serious offence is more likely to be jailed. For how long and where depends very much on the nature of the offence. In the case of 'aggravated murder', for instance, there is prescribed by law a minimum sentence of forty years' imprisonment, whereas for other types of murder the sentence is life imprisonment which is on average about fifteen years. Where a person is sent to complete a term of imprisonment depends on the age of the offender and the nature of the offence.

CRIMINAL INJURIES COMPENSATION SCHEME

Where a member of the public suffers personal injuries as a result of a crime of violence s/he may seek compensation from the state under this scheme. Originally, compensation was payable in respect of pain and suffering; however, since 1986 applicants are only entitled to recover actual out-of-pocket expenses such as hospital costs, loss of wages, etc.

The Criminal Justice Act, 1993 enables the Court of Criminal Appeal to review unduly lenient sentences, to make other provision in relation to sentencing and to provide for the payment by offenders of compensation for injury or loss resulting from their offences.

CUSTODY

Custody concerns the duty and responsibility of the day-to-day caring for a child.

When parents (who are married to each other) are living apart, custody can become a thorny issue. If the matter cannot be resolved by the parents and it comes before a court the principal concern of that court is the welfare of the child. Custody will be given to the parent who the court considers will best provide for the religious, moral, intellectual, physical, emotional and social well-being of the child. Generally, a mother is in a better position in custody cases where the children are young but there are exceptions to this. Custody orders are not final and may be changed or revoked upon an application to the court. They are effective until a child reaches eighteen years.

Where one parent is granted custody, then the other parent is usually granted access. Access is the right to see the children regularly so that a relationship may be formed with them. The form of access i.e. supervised, unsupervised, weekly, during holiday periods, etc. depends on each individual case. The parent who has access is still, however, a guardian and so must be consulted about the children's upbringing, education, trips abroad, etc.

Custody of Children Born Outside Marriage

Normally the mother of a child born outside marriage has sole custody of the child. The child is physically in her care and control. The father may apply to court for custody regardless of whether or not he was appointed guardian. Usually, natural fathers are not in a good position to obtain custody. Access may, however, be applied for.

DEATH

Death, that most tragic and final of events, leaves the family in a sad, numb and often very lonely condition. After the mourners have left, and the numerous visits have trickled to a few, the family must now face and deal with the legal consequences of their bereavement. The law, sometimes perceived as an unwelcome and expensive intruder, controls the procedures whereby the property of the deceased is passed on to whomsoever is entitled to receive it. Who is entitled to receive it?

There are many answers to this question. It is the intention here to set out the ones most commonly encountered. They are dealt with in turn.

Survivorship

This arises where property, both real and personal, is owned by two or more persons as joint tenants. Real property means freehold property while personal property means all other property including leasehold land. On the death of one co-owner or joint tenant, his interest passes automatically to the survivors.

The most frequently found situation is where a husband and wife own properties as joint tenants. If the husband dies first, the wife will own the entire property.

The essential document of proof is a death certificate, which can be obtained from the Registrar of Deaths, Births and Marriages, Lombard Street East, Dublin 2 or from the local County Council, once the death has been registered.

Registration of the death is effected by the transmission of a certificate of cause of death or the result of a coroner's inquest to the Registrar of Deaths.

Bank Account
Where the asset to be realised is the proceeds of a bank account, the production of the death certificate to the particular bank is normally sufficient. If the account is very large, the bank may not be prepared to transfer the account into the name of the survivor, without the production of the certificate of clearance from capital acquisition tax (*see* page 46).

Similar proofs apply to joint accounts in building societies, the Post Office, Prize Bonds, Credit Unions, Investment Accounts and so on.

Where the asset is a share in a public liability company, the production of the death certificate to the registrar of the company is sufficient to have the shares certificate placed in the name of the survivor.

Where the asset involved is a house or land, there are a few steps which need to be taken to put the title in order. If your title is registered in the Land Registry (*see* page 40), the register should be amended by a simple application to delete the name of the deceased owner from the register. The form of application is an affidavit which must exhibit the death certificate and include a request to amend the register.

In a case of an unregistered title (*see* page 40), all that strictly needs to be done is for the death certificate to be placed with the title deeds. However it is wiser to place an affidavit with the deeds, which should exhibit the death certificate, reconcile the identity with the deceased co-owner and include a statement to the effect that the joint tenancy had not been severed prior to the death of the former co-owner.

A difficulty may often arise in carrying out these procedures if the house is mortgaged and the title deeds are with a lending institution. In such a situation it would be necessary to involve a solicitor to take up the title deeds to make the required amendments to the title, as clearly the lending institution will not release their security direct to the borrower.

Trusts
The trust is of long and ancient origin and can be found in all legal jurisdictions in various forms. It grew up initially as a way to circumvent the strict rule of the common law.

The essential nature of a trust is that a person called a Settlor gives property to another person called a Trustee. The property is not for the benefit of the Trustee but rather for the good of a third person called the beneficiary.

Trusts can be in many and indeed very complicated forms, set up for reasons as varied as providing for one's mistress or co-habitee to avoiding income tax. The most common example, found principally among the farming community, arises where the owner of land (the Settlor), gives land to the Trustee to hold for the benefit of the Settlor's wife for her life and after her life for the eldest son absolutely.

The trust in this situation will come to an end when the wife dies at which time the son, called the Remainder Man, will be absolutely entitled. On the occurring of the event, i.e. the death of the wife, the Trustee will transfer the property into the son's name.

Will

A will is the document in which a person expresses his wishes as to how his property will be shared after his death.

This is a very simple document. It must be signed by the testator (i.e. the person making the will, testatrix being the female version) in the presence of two witnesses. Neither of the witnesses should be a beneficiary to the will for if they are this would render void any gift to them in the will, though it will not invalidate the rest of the will. The following is a standard simple form of Will.

THIS IS THE LAST WILL AND TESTAMENT of me JOSEPH CLAFFEY, OF 204 St Mungos Road, Dublin.

(1) I hereby revoke all former Wills or Codicils at any time heretofore made by me.

(2) I appoint as Executor and Trustee of this my Will my wife Carmel Claffey.

(3) I GIVE DEVISE AND BEQUEATH all of my property of every nature and kind whether real or personal and wheresoever situate and to which I shall die seized or possessed to my said wife Carmel Claffey for her own use and benefit absolutely.

IN WITNESS whereof I have hereunto set my hand this 17th day of March one thousand nine hundred and ninety two.

Joseph Claffey

SIGNED by the said JOSEPH CLAFFEY as and for his last Will and
Testament in the presence of us who in his presence and in the
presence of each other (all three being present at the same time)
have hereunto subscribed our names as witnesses.

Kieran Flannery	*Gerard Starr*
Solicitor	Solicitor's Apprentice
Dublin	Dublin

The will usually contains the appointment of an executor (female
executrix) whose duty it will be to prove the will and administer
the estate.

If no executor is appointed or the executor has predeceased
the testator, the estate will have to be administered by a person
called an administrator. This person will be the residuary legatee
and devisee (i.e. the person entitled to inherit the rest of the
estate after all the specific gifts have been dealt with). In a
situation where a Will fails to appoint an executor or residuary
legatee and devisee or they have died before the deceased, the
administrator will be the next-of-kin who will be ascertained by
reference to the Succession Act with which we shall deal later.

So when a person dies leaving a will what steps are required to
prove the will and administer the estate?

(1) The will must be located. With luck the intended executor
or some member of the deceased family will know of its
whereabouts. When one makes a will the proposed
executor should be informed of its whereabouts.

The likely place to find a will is at the home of the
deceased, the office of the deceased's solicitor, or with the
title deeds of the house in a bank, or in the old boot box on
top of the wardrobe.

(2) The next essential item is a death certificate which as we
already said can be obtained from the Registrar of Deaths,
Births and Marriages.

(3) The executor must now decide whether he will instruct a
solicitor to assist him in the administration of the estate and
proving the will or take on the chore himself through the
personal application section of the Probate Office. It will
obviously be more expensive to use a solicitor but of course

less troublesome as the solicitor will do most of the leg work in ascertaining the assets.

If the executor decides to prove the will himself he will have to apply to the Personal Applications Section of the Probate Office, Aras Ui Dhalaigh, Four Courts, Dublin, for an appointment. The staff of the Personal Applications Section have a tradition of being very helpful and will certainly give every assistance to the executor.

(4) The assets and liabilities of the estate must now be established: Bank statements, building society accounts, Post Office accounts, Prize Bonds, insurance policies, stocks and shares, land, houses, etc. Property held under a joint tenancy is not included for probate purposes, though it must be returned for capital acquisition tax purposes.

(5) A return to the Revenue Commissioners must be made setting out the assets and liabilities of the estate together with a Probate Tax Return form which was introduced by the 1993 Finance Act. This is done by way of a sworn affidavit in a form provided by the Revenue Commissioners. This affidavit must be completed with great care and honesty. The Revenue Commissioners will examine this document and may query valuations.

(6) A number of forms, including the original will, will now be lodged in the Probate Office where all the documents will be examined by the probate officials.

(7) If everything is in order the Probate Officer will give the executor a document called a Grant of Probate. The executor is now ready to administer the estate which we will deal with on page 68 after we have dealt with Intestacy, as the administration of the estate under will and under intestacy is similar.

Intestacy

This arises where someone dies without making a will or where there is a will but it fails to dispose of the entire estate. This latter situation is called partial intestacy.

The object of the exercise is similar to the will situation in that a document, in this case called a Grant of Administration, will ultimately be obtained from the Probate Office.

First we must discover who is entitled to apply for a Grant of Administration. The answer to this question is guided by the legal principle which states that the grant must follow the interest.

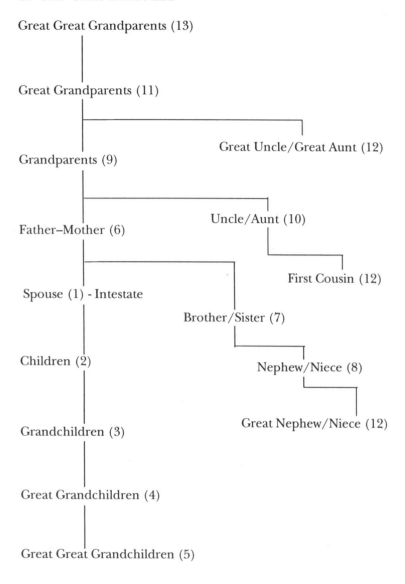

Great Great Grandparents (13)

Great Grandparents (11)

Grandparents (9)

Great Uncle/Great Aunt (12)

Father–Mother (6)

Uncle/Aunt (10)

First Cousin (12)

Spouse (1) - Intestate

Brother/Sister (7)

Children (2)

Nephew/Niece (8)

Grandchildren (3)

Great Nephew/Niece (12)

Great Grandchildren (4)

Great Great Grandchildren (5)

Basically this means that the person entitled to the lion's share of the estate is entitled to a first crack at taking out the Grant of Administration.

The most common situation which arises is that a husband often dies survived by his wife and children. In this case his wife is entitled to take out the Grant of Administration.

In a situation where a wife has predeceased him and he is survived by his children only, here any member of the family may take out the Grant of Administration. In this case if the children are under the age of eighteen, i.e. the legal age of majority, the Probate Office will issue a limited grant of administration to some adult member of the family, generally an aunt or uncle. This can only be used until the eldest child reaches eighteen, when it must be surrendered. Then a new full grant will issue to the child who has attained his majority.

In the case where a person dies either single or widowed leaving no children that person's parents are entitled to take out the grant.

The diagram (on page 66) establishes who is entitled to take out the grant and their order of entitlement.

Having ascertained who the administrator will be, we must now get ready to extract the grant. The procedure is quite similar to that in which one proves a will with one exception. By virtue of the fact that an administrator is not appointed by the testator, the courts insist that a bond be entered into by the administrator with the President of the High Court that the administrator will administer the estate correctly and distribute the assets to the proper beneficiaries.

The bond will have the administrator as the primary surety but it will also have a second surety which may be an insurance company or some other person who is willing to swear that his assets are equivalent to half the estate of the deceased.

Having extracted the Grant of Administration the administrator must now distribute the estate according to the provisions of the Succession Act. The most common entitlements arise in the following situations. Where a person dies leaving a spouse and children, the spouse is entitled to two-thirds of the estate and the children are entitled to one-third of the estate.

In the situation where the person dies leaving a spouse and no children then the spouse is entitled to the entire estate.

If a spouse dies a widower or widow leaving children then the children are entitled to the estate in equal shares.

In that last situation if any of the children had died, leaving children themselves, these children being the grandchildren of the deceased are entitled to take their parents' share. This is known as the per stirpes rule which can be explained with the following diagram:

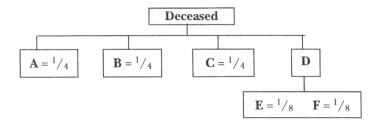

As one can see the beneficiaries are not of equal degree. The deceased had four children so his estate should be divided into four equal parts. A, B and C in the diagram get one quarter each. However, D having predeceased the deceased his share will be divided between his children E and F who will take a one-eighth share each. In this situation, if D left no issue, the share of A, B and C would increase to one-third each.

Administration on the Estate

First we must look at the power of the executor/administrator which is similar when an executor/administrator has a year from the date of death in which to carry out his duties. He basically acts as trustee of the estate, and the relationship with the beneficiaries is similar to that of trustee. An executor must implement the terms of the will. He must be very careful, as the Succession Act places certain restrictions on the power of a person to make dispositions. The principal restraints are:

(1) The spouse's legal right. When a person is making his will he must make provision for his spouse. If there are no children of the family, the spouse must get one-half of the estate. If there are children the spouse must get a one-third share. In a case where the will disobeys this stipulation, the executor must serve notices on the spouse so that the spouse has an opportunity to assert her/his right.

(2) There is an encouragement in Section 117 of the Succession Act that a testator should provide for his children. The ambit of this section is established by case law, and will very much depend on any individual case. The principle urges that one should make provision for one's children as a just and prudent parent would. The onus is on the disappointed child to assert this right which he must do within one year of the issue of the Grant of Probate. If an

executor felt he was likely to be met with an application under this section he would be very unwise to distribute the estate until the extent of the claim had been ascertained.

(3) Under Section 56 of the Succession Act a surviving spouse of a deceased person has a right to require appropriation of the family dwelling and household chattels in satisfaction of her share. It is the duty of the administrator/executor to notify the surviving spouse in writing of her rights under this section, and the spouse will have a period of six months from receipt of written notification or one year from the date of Grant of Probate or administration in which to exercise the right. Where the dwelling house and chattels are worth more than the share to which the spouse is entitled he or she may have to make up the balance in cash in order to exercise the option. There are certain circumstances in which the spouse will be entitled to apply to the court to have the dwelling and household chattels appropriated either *(a)* without payment of the money necessary to make up the difference between the share and the value of property or *(b)* subject to the payment of such sum as the court may consider reasonable. The court will be guided by the likelihood of hardship being suffered by the surviving spouse and also by any infant children.

(4) There is also provision in Section 120 of the Succession Act which relates to a person's unworthiness to succeed. A sane person who has been guilty of murder or attempted murder or manslaughter of another shall be precluded from taking any share in the estate of that other person. Also a spouse against whom a deceased obtained a decree of divorce *a mensa et toro* — a court order which permits the parties to live apart but not to remarry — or a spouse who failed to comply with a decree for the restitution of conjugal rights obtained by the deceased, or a spouse guilty of desertion for two years or more immediately prior to the death of the deceased is precluded from taking any share in the estate either on intestacy or as a legal right. Likewise a person who has been found guilty of an offence against the deceased or against the spouse or any child of the deceased which is punishable by imprisonment for a maximum term of at least two years or by a more severe penalty shall also be

precluded from taking any share in the estate of the deceased as a legal right or for making an application under Section 117.

Steps to be Taken by the Executor and Administrator

(1) The executor will now realise all the assets and convert them into cash where applicable.

(2) He will discharge all the debts of the deceased. Secure creditors, for example, the owner of a legal mortgage over property must be paid first followed by the preferential creditors and so on. An executor/administrator will secure statutory protection for himself by inserting an advertisement in the paper for creditors. When the notice giving this advertisement has expired he may now pay out the shares under the intestacy, or pay out the gifts set out in the will. Specific gifts must be paid first as they rank in priority to the residuary bequests. If there are insufficient funds in the estate to discharge all the specific requests they will have to abate proportionately. In relation to real property, i.e. houses and farms, *see* page 44.

DEFAMATION

A defamatory statement is a false statement which injures the reputation of the Plaintiff by its tendency to 'lower him in the estimation of right thinking members of society' or to cause right thinking members of society 'to shun or avoid' him. The task presented to the law is to adjudicate between two competing interests, firstly the right of free speech and secondly the right of the individual to preserve his reputation from unjust attack. There are two forms of defamation, libel and slander. The difference between them is as follows:

Libel is where the defamation is in permanent form, such as a statue, a film, a written record, and it is actionable *per se*, i.e. without proof of damage. Finally, it may be a crime, as in seditious or obscene libel.

On the other hand, *slander* is in non-permanent form and cannot be a crime. It is actionable only on proof of special damage, i.e. damage capable of being expressed in terms of money except in the following four circumstances:

(1) If it is imputed that the Plaintiff had committed a crime punishable by death or imprisonment.

(2) If it is imputed that the Plaintiff had an existing contagious or infectious disease.

(3) If it is imputed that a female had committed adultery or was not chaste.

(4) If statements are made about the Plaintiff 'calculated to disparage him in any office, profession, calling, trade or business held or carried on by him at the time of the publication'.

It is not enough that the defamatory statement be made. There must be publication: that means communication to a third party. Language is the usual form of publication but any method by which meaning can be communicated will be sufficient. Section 14(2) of the Defamation Act, 1961 provides that: 'Any reference in this part to words shall be construed as including a reference to visual images, gestures and other methods of signifying meaning.'

Defamation should be distinguished from the following:

(a) Mere vulgar abuse which injures a person's dignity only and not his reputation: *Penfold* v. *Westcote* (1806): 'You blackguard, rascal, scoundrel, Penfold you are a thief.' It was held by the court that 'Blackguard' etc. was mere abuse but was defamatory in conjunction with 'thief'.

(b) Injurious falsehood. A statement is not defamatory unless it injures the person's reputation, e.g. a statement which injures his business but not his personal reputation is actionable (if at all) as injurious falsehood. An injurious falsehood may be defined as a false statement made maliciously about a person or his property or goods so that other persons are deceived with consequential damage to the Plaintiff.

Should a defamation action proceed to hearing, it will be necessary for the Plaintiff to show proof of the following: that the statement was defamatory; that the statement referred to the Plaintiff; and that the statement was published.

At this juncture it is appropriate to look at the functions of judge and jury. The judge's function is to decide as a matter of law whether the statement is reasonably capable of bearing the defamatory meaning alleged by the Plaintiff. If not so satisfied, the case is withheld from the jury. However, if the judge decides that the words are capable of such defamatory meaning, then it is for the jury to decide whether the words in fact have a defamatory meaning. The Defendant may deny that the matter complained of is defamatory or deny publication. Other defences that may be availed of are: justification, fair comment, privilege absolute and qualified, offer of amends, apology and, finally, consent.

A word about each of the Defences

The Defendant may deny that the matter complained of is defamatory; however, as mentioned above, it is for the judge to decide if the matter complained of is capable of bearing the defamatory meaning alleged by the Plaintiff. If the judge decides, the matter then goes to the jury. The Defendant's evidence will have to be strong to refute the allegation. It is also up to the Defendant to deny publication. To be published, a statement must be made known to at least one person other than the person defamed. Publication need not be to the public at large. A statement is not published unless understood. A person to whom an allegedly defamatory statement is published must understand:

 (*a*) its meaning, and

 (*b*) that it refers to the Plaintiff.

Justification consists of proof that the allegedly defamatory matter was true. Justification is a dangerous defence because, if it fails, exemplary damages will probably be awarded. In justification, the Defendant must prove that the statement was true and it is sufficient to prove the substantial truth of the statement. That is, a minor inaccuracy will not set aside the defence; it is the jury's task to decide whether the inaccuracy was minor or otherwise.

Fair comment is comment honestly made on a matter of public interest. An essential of fair comment is that the defendant must have made it in good faith, that is believing in its truth and without malicious distortion. In addition, the Defendant must prove that the matter commented on was one of public interest.

Defendants often plead *privilege*. A privileged communication may be defined as one in respect of which the law holds that the public interest in free speech overrides the private right to an untarnished reputation. Privilege may be either absolute or qualified. Absolute privilege is not actionable under any circumstances and qualified privilege is actionable only on proof of express malice. The Supreme Court made a ruling recently on government cabinet confidentiality. It decided that cabinet confidentiality is, in fact, absolute. For a statement to enjoy qualified privilege, there must be a legal, moral or social duty to make it on one side and a corresponding interest to receive it on the other. Both these conditions must be satisfied.

Section 21 of the Defamation Act, 1961 makes provision for an *offer of amends* in the case of unintentional defamation. Section 17 of the Defamation Act, 1961 provides that an offer by the Defendant of an *apology*, made before the commencement of the action or as soon afterwards as he had an opportunity of doing so, if the action was commenced before the Defendant had an opportunity of apologising, shall be admissible as evidence in mitigation of damages. The apology made must be a genuine apology and if the court is of the opinion that it is insincere it may reject it.

As regards *consent*, it is a defence that the Plaintiff gave express or implied consent to the allegedly defamatory publication. In some instances the Defendant may seek to argue that, although the consent was not expressly made by the Plaintiff, it can be implied from an examination of the circumstances of the case. Either way, the consent of the Plaintiff must be real.

DIVORCE

'No law shall be enacted providing for the grant of a dissolution of marriage.' Art. 41.3.2 Constitution.

It is not possible to get a divorce in an Irish court because of the constitutional ban. However, Irish courts do, in certain circumstances, recognise divorces granted by courts in other countries. This recognition depends on the law of domicile.

Domicile means residing in a country with the intention of living there permanently or indefinitely. This is known as 'domicile of choice' and can only be acquired by a person over eighteen years. A minor's domicile (under eighteen) is a domicile of dependence and is determined by the parents' domicile. This means that if a minor is living in Ireland but his/her parents are domiciled in Australia then that minor has an Australian domicile. Before October 1986 a married woman's domicile was that of her husband. If her husband moved to England and decided to stay there while she continued to live in Ireland she was considered legally to be domiciled in England. So if he obtained a divorce in England it would be recognised here. If, however, the situation was reversed with the wife moving permanently to England and obtaining a divorce while the husband remained in Ireland, then that divorce would not be recognised as she would be deemed to be domiciled in Ireland where there is no divorce law.

With the abolition of the married woman's dependent domicile in October 1986, under the Domicile and Recognition of Foreign Divorces Act, the situation changed somewhat. For divorces granted after 2 October 1986, the rule is that the divorce will be recognised here if either of the spouses is domiciled in the country granting it. The act did not have retrospective effect. However, in a 1991 case the High Court questioned the constitutionality of the married woman's 'domicile of dependency'. The judge was of the opinion that married women could always have their own independent domicile. The Supreme Court decided on this issue in December 1992. It held that the pre-1986 rule, that a woman acquired on marriage the domicile of her husband, was unconstitutional. Divorces granted before 1986 in a foreign country in which either the husband or wife was domiciled at the time of the divorce proceedings will be recognised in Ireland.

It must be stated again that to establish domicile you must prove residence and clearly show an intention to remain there permanently or indefinitely. The setting up of a mailing address does not establish domicile.

DOGS

No matter how much you love and care for your dog you must have a licence for it. A licence may be purchased for £5 at any Post Office and lasts for one year.

The family dog and, indeed, the working dog can be a source of great comfort, companionship and help but, if not properly controlled, dogs can be a source of embarrassment or even of costly and time consuming litigation. A recent Supreme Court decision held that an owner of a dog is liable to a person bitten by that dog when it is shown that the dog had displayed a vicious propensity (an inclination or a predisposition to do something) and might bite someone. It is not necessary to show that the dog *will* bite someone. In the case just mentioned, a seven-year-old girl was attacked by a mongrel Alsatian while she was in the foyer of a hotel to use its leisure facilities. She sued both the owner of the dog and the hotel manager for negligence and breach of duty, including breach of statutory duty in and about the management and maintenance of the hotel and the keeping and training of dogs. She alleged that, on the date she was attacked and on other dates, the dog had exhibited a mischievous and/or a vicious propensity and that this was a fact which both Defendants knew or ought to have known.

The Supreme Court indicated that one does not have to wait for the growling and frightened dog to bite somebody in order to know that it might do so. It is sufficient to establish that the dog *may* bite someone and not that it *will* bite someone.

In this case, the animal was allowed to roam within a building. It is therefore necessary that your dog should not wander about without supervision or control, whether within or without a building. Some time ago the Minister for Justice made an order concerning certain breeds and their control and supervision when in public. The twelve breeds of dogs which must now be muzzled are: American Pit Bull Terriers, English Bull Terriers, Staffordshire Bull Terriers, Bandogs, Bulldogs, Bull Mastiffs, Dobermann Pinscher, German Shepherd, Rhodesian Ridgeback, Rotweiler, Japanese Akita and Japanese Tosas. The order was made as a result of a number of incidents involving Rotweilers, which attacked people, and pitbull terriers among others. Among the rules concerning the dogs listed in the order are the following:

(1) the animal must be accompanied by a person who is sixteen years of age, or older, and who is capable of controlling the dog;

(2) the dog must be wearing a collar with its name and the address of the owner on a badge or disc;

(3)   the dog must be securely muzzled;

(4) the dog must be led by a leash that does not exceed a certain length.

A word, in turn, about barking dogs, guard dogs and dogs found roaming on farms, especially during lambing or calving time. Persons who suffer from insomnia would not be helped by a barking dog and such barking can, in fact, be looked upon as a nuisance.

Whether a person is the owner or tenant of property, that person is entitled to enjoy the premises in comfort and if a dog barks at a late hour it is interfering with that enjoyment and comfort. The best approach is dialogue to see if the dog's owner can control its barking. Failing that, it may be necessary to make a complaint to the appropriate authority, either to a dog warden or the District Court. A once-off situation will not be sufficient to warrant the making of a Court Order. It would require a series of barkings going on over a period of time. If the owner of barking dogs has a large number of them, it would be open to the Court to limit this number bearing in mind the size of the garden and house and the general neighbourhood. In this instance, failure to obey the Court Order might result in contempt proceedings.

Security Firms

Under the Control of Dogs Act, 1986 (Section 25), Security firms who provide guard dog services are under an obligation to make sure that the dog or dogs are not roaming the premises being protected. As already mentioned in an earlier chapter, people come on premises either as invitees, licensees or trespassers and the owner or occupier owes a duty to each in turn. The security firm would be well advised to make sure that the animal can carry out the work intended without being a danger to any one of the three. It would also be advisable to place at appropriate entrances, etc. notices to the effect that guard dogs are on the premises. The guard dog in question must also have a special identification which is, in fact, placed under the skin as a permanent means of identification.

Stray Dogs

Finally, farmers are extremely concerned at lambing and calving time that their flocks or herds might be attacked by either a single dog or dogs roaming in packs. It will be a good defence if a farmer can show that he genuinely believed that the dog, or pack of dogs, was worrying his sheep or cattle and that he took the appropriate action by shooting the offending dogs.

DOMICILE

Domicile affects, among other things, the validity of wills, distribution of property on intestacy, capacity to marry and recognition of foreign divorces. Every person has a domicile and no person can have more than one at any one time.

A person's domicile is said to be that place in which he has his permanent home. The concept of domicile involves two elements:

(*i*) actual residence *and*

(*ii*) the intention to remain there permanently or indefinitely. Where residence and intention concur, there is domicile. There are three classes of domicile:

Domicile of Origin

This attaches at a person's birth. A child born within a marriage takes the domicile of the father; a non-marital child that of its mother. As you can see, intention is not a feature of domicile of origin. A domicile of origin cannot be entirely lost or extinguished.

Domicile of Choice

Where a person of full age and sound mind leaves the country of his domicile of origin and takes up residence in another country, with the intention of living there permanently or at least indefinitely, he is regarded as having acquired a domicile of choice. A further change of residence and intention will again affect domicile. A new domicile of choice may be acquired or where there is no definite intention to live in a place permanently or indefinitely the domicile of origin is established.

Length of residence in a place is not of itself a determining factor in establishing domicile as the example below will indicate:

> *A man left his home in State X and took his family to a house in State Y, about half a mile from X, intending to live there permanently. Having left his belongings there, he and his family returned to X to spend the night with a relative. He became ill and died. It was held that his domicile at death was in Y.*

Domicile of Dependency

Unmarried minors (under eighteen years of age) and persons of unsound mind have what is known as domicile of dependence. They take the domicile of the appropriate parent (*see* above). Until the coming into force of the Domicile and Recognition of Foreign Divorces Act, 1986, a married woman's domicile was one of dependency. She acquired her husband's domicile upon marriage and during that marriage was unable to acquire an independent domicile of her own. This meant that if a husband left his wife, went to England and decided to stay there, even though his wife was still living in Ireland, she was regarded legally as being domiciled in England. However, if she went to England never to return and, for example, subsequently obtained a divorce there, the divorce could not be recognised as she would be deemed to be domiciled with her husband, i.e. in Ireland.

Since 2 October 1986 this no longer applies and a married woman can now acquire her own independent domicile.

A further development took place in December 1992 when the Supreme Court in a four-to-one majority ruled unconstitutional the pre-1986 rule that the domicile of a married woman was the same as that of her husband. One judge described it as a 'relic of matrimonial female bondage'. That decision effectively made the 1986 legislation retrospective (*see* DIVORCE).

DRIVING OFFENCES

In this chapter it is intended to deal with dangerous driving, careless driving, inconsiderate driving and drink driving. The use of the motor car has brought many benefits to mankind but its misuse has been the cause of much misery and inconvenience.

Dangerous Driving

The Road Traffic Acts of 1961 and 1968 provide that 'A person shall not drive a vehicle in a public place in a manner (including speed) which having regard to all the circumstances of the case (including the condition of the vehicle, the nature, condition and use of the place and the amount of traffic which then actually is or might reasonably be expected then to be therein) is dangerous to the public.'

The 1961 Road Traffic Act created two offences: driving 'in a manner' or driving 'at a speed' dangerous to the public. The 1961 Act was challenged and the section was amended by the 1968 Act. Today the offence of driving 'in a manner' dangerous to the public remains, but the courts, in deciding the manner of driving, may look at the speed. In addition to the speed, the court may take all circumstances into consideration. This means that the condition of the vehicle, the nature of the place, the condition of the place, and the amount of traffic actually on the highway at the time of the alleged offence may be taken into consideration. 'Dangerous to the public' was viewed as driving in a manner which involved, unjustifiably, definite risk of harm to the public. The penalties where death or serious bodily harm to another results, is a fine not exceeding £3,000 and/or a term not exceeding five years' penal servitude. The penalty for dangerous driving on conviction is a fine not exceeding £1,000 and/or a term of imprisonment not exceeding six months.

Careless Driving

This consists of a person driving a vehicle in a public place without due care and attention. A notice of intention to prosecute is necessary in respect of a number of offences under the Road Traffic Act (1961). This is, in effect a preliminary warning to the driver that a prosecution may follow. The purpose is to give the accused notice of a possible prosecution while the events are still fresh in his mind. This warning must be properly served to the satisfaction of the court; otherwise, any prosecution may fail.

There are four ways in which the warning may be given:
  (1) A notice in writing stating all the particulars, for example, the time and place of the alleged offence and the intention to prosecute. This may be served personally or by registered post on the accused.
  (2) By verbal warning.
  (3) By service of the summons for the alleged offence within fourteen days of its commission.
  (4) By waiver.

The waiver provides a number of situations where failure to serve a Notice of Intention to prosecute is not a bar on conviction. The penalty on conviction is a fine not exceeding £350 and/or imprisonment for a maximum of three months.

Inconsiderate Driving

This consists of a person driving a vehicle in a public place without reasonable consideration for other persons using the place. This is a lesser offence than careless driving. It is for the court to decide what constitutes 'without reasonable consideration for other persons using the place'. The penalty on conviction for the first offence is a fine of £150 maximum; second and subsequent offences, £350 and/or three months' imprisonment. Again, a Notice of Intention to prosecute is necessary under the 1961 Act.

Drunk Driving

There is a prohibition on driving a mechanically propelled vehicle while under the influence of an intoxicant. An intoxicant includes alcohol and drugs and any combination of drugs and alcohol. Driving, or attempting to drive, in charge, driving an animal drawn vehicle or pedal cycle, and being found in a public place under the influence of liquor or drugs are the principal sections which come under the heading 'capacity offences'.

It is a matter of evidence if a person does not have proper control due to the influence of an intoxicant. If a garda is of the opinion that a person has committed an offence under any of the above sections he may arrest the person without warrant. He must, however, give the reason for the arrest. The arrest must be clear and unambiguous. If a garda is satisfied that an offence has been committed he is obliged to give the caution, that is, the suspect motorist is not bound to say anything or anything he does say may be taken down in writing and may be given in evidence. The suspect motorist is then taken to a garda station. A garda medical doctor may be called with the view to carry out an examination but the suspect motorist is not obliged to submit to the examination. It is not an offence to refuse a medical examination, unlike the refusal of scientific tests. If the suspect motorist consents to a medical examination, the garda medical doctor will carry out a detailed test to ascertain mental alertness, physical condition, reflexes, etc. In due course the suspect motorist is allowed home. A charge will be heard in the District Court and, if convicted, it is open to him to appeal the decision to the Circuit Court where there is a complete re-hearing.

Today the scientific tests—that is, the blood or urine sample —have largely replaced the capacity test. Under this scientific approach, a garda who forms the opinion that liquor has been consumed may require a motorist to give a specimen of breath. Whether a specimen of breath is given or not it is open to the garda to arrest without warrant and to require the suspect motorist to give a specimen of blood or urine to a garda medical doctor. There are statutory and regulatory provisions which a garda and the doctor and the medical bureau of road safety are obliged to follow. The permitted limit is 100 mg of alcohol per 100 ml of blood, which corresponds roughly to just over two pints of beer or three small whiskies. If the concentration of alcohol is above the permitted limit, the motorist will be convicted and may face a penalty of up to £1,000 and twelve months' disqualification from driving.

Today the scientific test or analysis test is now more favoured precisely because it is 'science' based rather than 'opinion' based. In the capacity test, great reliance was placed on medical and other evidence and in some instances there was no medical evidence and the courts were therefore obliged to rely on non-professional witness observations.

EC LAW

The primary sources of EC law are to be found in the following treaties:

(*a*) European Coal and Steel Community Treaty, 1951.

(*b*) European Economic Treaty, 1957 (Treaty of Rome).

(*c*) Euratom Treaty, 1957 (atomic energy).

(*d*) Convention on Certain Institutions Common to the European Communities, 1957.

(*e*) Merger Treaty, 1965.

(*f*) Acts of Accession of 1972 (UK, Ireland, Denmark), 1979; (Greece), 1985.

(*g*) Budgetary Treaties of 1970 and 1975.

(*h*) The Treaty amending the Treaties establishing the Community with respect to Greenland, 1985.

(*i*) Single European Act, 1986.

(*j*) Maastricht Treaty 1992.

As the primary sources, these treaties may be described as the constitution of the Community. Any legislation passed by the institutions of the Community (the Commission and the Council of Ministers) must not contradict these Treaties.

The *Commission* consists of seventeen members (two each from Germany, France, Italy, Spain and the UK and one each from the other member states) appointed by agreement of the governments of the member states. The President of the Commission holds office for a renewable term of two years. The Commission has a four-year term of office which is also renewable.

The *Council of Ministers* is not a fixed body but is made up of ministers/representatives from the governments of each member state with membership depending on the issues under discussion e.g. agriculture, fisheries, employment, etc. Presidency of the Council rotates in alphabetical order every six months. Britain held this position in the latter half of 1992.

It is the Commission and the Council of Ministers who are empowered to pass legislation to achieve the objectives of the Treaties. Such legislation takes the form of Regulations, Directives or Decisions.

Regulations

A regulation sets out general rules which apply uniformly throughout the EC. It is binding in its entirety and directly applicable in all member states without the need for further legislation. An example of a Regulation is Regulation no. 1612/68 on Freedom of Movement.

Directives
A directive is binding upon the member state to which it is addressed as to the result to be achieved. A member state is therefore allowed a discretion as to the means of implementing a directive. Directive 75/117 on the application of the principle of equal pay for men and women or the Directive of 3 May 1988 on the approximation of the laws of the member states concerning the safety of toys are examples. Ireland's Anti-Discrimination (Pay) Act, 1974 gave effect to Directive 75/117.

Decisions
A decision is addressed to specified persons, companies or member states and is legally binding in its entirety on those to whom it is addressed. A Commission decision that a company is infringing competition rules is an example.

EMPLOYMENT EQUALITY LEGISLATION
Irish employment equality legislation, as found in the Anti-Discrimination (Pay) Act, 1974 and the Employment Equality Act, 1977, derives mainly from EC directives on equal pay and equality of treatment for men and women which give effect to Articles 119 and 235 of the Treaty of Rome.

Anti-Discrimination (Pay) Act, 1974
This Act applies to all employees including temporary and part-time. It provides for equal pay between men and women, if they are doing like work. Pay is taken in its broadest definition and is defined as including

> any consideration, whether in cash or in kind, which an employee receives directly or indirectly in respect of his employment from his employer.

This has been interpreted as including bonus payments, pensions, marriage gratuities, overtime payments, house purchase loans, commission on sales, sick pay and even special travel concessions for retired employees.

The principle of equal pay for like work has been introduced into Irish law by this Act, but how do we define like work? Two persons are regarded as employed on like work where

(i) Both perform the same work under the same or similar conditions, or where each is in every respect interchangeable with the other in relation to the work *or*

(ii) Where the work performed by one is similar to that performed by the other and any differences between the work performed or the conditions under which it is performed by each occur only infrequently or are of small importance in relation to the work as a whole *or*

(iii) Where the work performed by one is equal in value to that performed by the other in the demands it makes on skill, physical and mental effort, responsibility and working conditions. (This could cover situations where the work and working conditions of the employees involved are totally different e.g. a factory worker and an office worker.)

Most claims under the Act are based on the grounds set out at *(iii)* above.

Section 2(3) allows an employer to pay different rates of remuneration for like work on grounds other than sex provided that the reason is genuine and not merely a pretext for discrimination. Previous experience and training are examples of such grounds but these are not exhaustive and it is anticipated that there will be further interpretations.

Claims

An equal pay claim should first be made to the employer. If this is unsuccessful then the claim may be brought to an Equality Officer. The Equality Officer is obliged to investigate and issue a recommendation. Either party to the dispute may then appeal that decision to the Labour Court not later than forty-two days after the date of the Equality Officer's recommendation.

Where a person is in breach of this Act a procedure exists whereby that person may be prosecuted and fined up to £100 plus £10 for each day the offence continues. A fine payable to the injured party may also be imposed.

A claim under this Act must be based on a comparison between men and women working for the *same employer* or an *associated employer* i.e. where one firm controls another or both are controlled by a third. The men and women must also be working in the 'same place'. The same place includes a city, town or locality and not just the same factory or office.

Employment Equality Act, 1977

This Act makes it illegal for an employer to discriminate on grounds of sex or marital status in employment. Employers are forbidden to discriminate in relation to access to employment, conditions of employment other than pay, training, promotion, regrading and pensions.

All employees are protected by this Act except those limited cases where the sex of the person is an occupational qualification. Examples include:

- where on grounds of physiology (excluding physical strength or stamina) or on the grounds of authenticity for the purpose of entertainment a member of a particular sex is required e.g. models, actors.
- where the posts are in the Prison Service or Garda Siochana and it is necessary that the posts are filled by persons of a particular sex. This necessity arises where the duties involve the carrying out of personal searches or the supervising of prisoners while they are dressing etc.

Selection of a candidate for a job cannot be based on the candidate's sex or marital status or on a requirement which is inessential for the performance of the job and which would constitute indirect discrimination e.g. an inessential qualification that may not have been open to males/females in the past. Limiting interviews to those of a particular sex or marital status or instructing interviewers not to employ persons of a particular sex or marital status is prohibited. Questions (at interviews) relating to how many children the applicant has, what child minding arrangements have been made, how the applicant would mix in an all male/female environment have been deemed to be unlawful.

Employers are forbidden to discriminate in respect of conditions of employment. This covers all aspects of the job: the physical working conditions, hours of work, overtime, transfers, dismissals, etc. It also concerns such matters as sexual harassment. Sexual harassment is behaviour of a sexual nature which is unwelcome to the recipient. It may consist of suggestive remarks, jokes, touching or even the display of pornographic material in the workplace. Where an employer is aware of such harassment, or should have been aware and did nothing about it, that employer may be held liable.

In relation to training or promotion, employers should not

assume that employees of a particular sex or marital status are not interested. This is discriminatory.

Positive discrimination is permitted under the Act. Employers and training organisations are allowed to encourage members of either sex to go into non-traditional areas of work. They are also allowed to arrange for or provide special treatment to women in relation to pregnancy or childbirth.

Taking a Claim

A claim should first be taken up with the employer. If this is not successful then the matter may, within six months, be referred to the Labour Court. The Labour Court may refer the matter to an Industrial Relations Officer or more usually to an Equality Officer who is obliged to investigate it and issue a recommendation. That decision may be appealed to the Labour Court. The Labour Court may recommend a specified course of action or award up to 104 weeks' pay. A prosecution may also follow with possible fines of up to £100 plus £10 for each day the offence continues.

Employment Equality Agency

This agency acts as a watchdog in the area of discrimination. It consists of a chairman and ten members representing various interest groups including the trade unions, employers' and women's organisations. The members are appointed by the Minister for Labour. The main duties of the Agency are:

- to promote equality of opportunity between men and women in relation to employment;
- to work towards the elimination of discrimination in employment;
- to review the operation of the equality legislation.

In addition to these duties it conducts and sponsors research and reports to the Minister. It can and does take legal action against organisations and people who practise discrimination and it also helps individuals who have suffered discrimination.

FIREARMS

Since the passing of the Firearms and Offensive Weapons Act, 1990 the definition of a firearm has been considerably widened. It includes the following:

(*a*) a lethal firearm or other lethal weapon of any description from which any shot, bullet or other missile can be discharged;

(b) an air gun;

(c) a crossbow;

(d) a type of stun gun or any other weapon for causing any shock to a person by means of electricity or any other kind of energy emission;

(e) a prohibited weapon i.e. a weapon designed to discharge noxious liquid gas or other noxious thing;

(f) certain telescope sights;

(g) certain silencers.

Possessing a firearm without a firearms certificate is an offence and carries a maximum penalty on summary conviction of a fine of £200 and/or one year's imprisonment and on indictment, a fine of £500 and/or five years' imprisonment. Obviously, there are many exceptions to this and they include army personnel and gardaí acting in the course of duty; members of authorised gun clubs; gillies; persons authorised to conduct theatre or cinema rehearsals and persons who slaughter animals using humane killers.

Firearms certificates are granted mainly by a garda superintendent. They are renewable annually. Applicants must be at least sixteen years of age and of sound mind and good character. There must be a genuine reason for requiring the firearm.

Possessing a firearm with intent to endanger life or cause injury to property, or enable any other person to so do, carries a maximum penalty of imprisonment for life.

Possessing a firearm or an imitation firearm with the intention of committing a serious offence or resisting arrest carries a maximum penalty of imprisonment for fourteen years. Possessing a firearm or imitation firearm while stealing a motor vehicle carries a maximum penalty of fourteen years.

GARDA CUSTODY

The manner in which persons held in custody are to be treated is governed by the Criminal Justice Act, 1984 (Treatment of Persons in Custody in Garda Síochána Stations) Regulations, 1987.

A *Custody Record* is kept in respect of each person held in custody. The information contained therein should include the following:

- the date, time and place of arrest;
- the identity of the person/garda who made the arrest;
- the time of arrival at the station;
- reason for the arrest;
- any relevant particulars relating to the detainee's physical or mental condition;
- visits to that person by gardaí;
- any other visits;
- enquiries concerning them;
- telephone calls made or letters sent by them;
- any requests made by them;
- meals supplied;
- the ending of the custody (release, station bail, etc.).

Custody records must be preserved for at least twelve months, longer if there is a complaint pending.

Information to be given to a person in custody
An arrested person will be informed of the following:
- the offence for which s/he has been arrested;
- that s/he may consult a solicitor in private;
- that s/he may have another person informed of the arrest;
- if the person is under seventeen years, that a parent, guardian or spouse will be notified of the arrest and asked to attend the station.

Information is also given on entitlement to visits, bail, and on procedures relating to searches, fingerprinting, identification parades, etc. This information is given in written form.

The detainee will be asked to sign the custody record on being given this information.

If the arrested person is a foreign national s/he may communicate with his/her consul.

Where the arrested person is charged with an offence a copy of the charge sheet containing particulars of the offence must be given to him/her. In the case of a person under seventeen years a copy will also be given to a parent or guardian. The copy must be signed for in the custody record.

Search on Arrest
There is an automatic right to search an arrested person and to take articles which are believed to be connected with the offence charged or with some other offence or which might be used by the detainee to injure persons or property or to effect an escape.

It is a limited power.

Various Acts give wider power of search, many without warrant. The main ones are:

The Misuse of Drugs Act, 1977 (S.23)

Criminal Law Act, 1976 (S.8)

Criminal Justice Act, 1984 (S.4,6)

Offences Against the State Act, 1939 (S.30).

Manners of Search

A person in custody must not be searched by a person (other than a doctor) of the opposite sex.

Where a search involves removal of clothing other than outdoor clothing (headgear, coat, gloves) no person of the opposite sex should be present unless that person is a doctor or his/her presence is required because of the violent conduct of the person to be searched.

A search involving removal of underclothing should, where practicable, be carried out by a doctor. Details of the search must be recorded including the name of the person conducting the search, the names of those present and particulars of any property taken. Any property taken must be signed for by the person searched.

Fingerprints, palm prints, photographs, swabs or samples may not be taken unless:

– the person gives his/her *written* consent;

– where the person is under seventeen years there is the written consent of an appropriate adult;

– power to do so has been granted by law. S.4 Criminal Justice Act, 1984 and S.30 Offences Against the State Act, 1939 grant such power.

Additional Garda Powers

Additional powers are given to the gardaí where persons are detained under S.4 Criminal Justice Act, 1984 or S.30 Offences Against the State Act, 1939. Generally the purpose of an arrest is to bring a person before a court. However, in the two situations above, a power is given to arrest and detain for the purpose of investigating the commission or suspected commission of a crime by the person arrested.

S.4 applies to offences (or attempts) which are punishable by imprisonment for a term of five years or more, e.g. murder. S.30 applies to offences which undermine public order, undermine the authority of the state and also to a catalogue of offences known as scheduled offences which of themselves are not necessarily subversive, e.g. serious assault or malicious damage.

Where a garda arrests a person whom s/he with reasonable cause suspects of having committed an offence to which these sections apply, that person may be detained in a garda station if the garda in charge of the station has, at the time of that person's arrival, reasonable grounds for believing that his/her detention is necessary for the proper investigation of the offence.

The period of detention should not exceed six hours. In the case of S.4, however, a garda not below the rank of superintendent may extend this for a further six hours if s/he has reasonable grounds for believing that such extension is necessary. If the person is being held under S.30 then the initial period of detention is twenty-four hours with an extension of twenty-four hours.

A garda may

(a) demand of him/her his/her name and address;

(b) carry out a search;

(c) seize and retain for testing anything that he/she has in his/her possession and, on the authority of a garda not below the rank of superintendent, a garda may

(d) cause him/her to be photographed;

(e) have fingerprints and palm prints taken
and, on the authority of a garda not below the rank of superintendent, a garda who with reasonable cause suspects that the detainee has concealed on his/her person a controlled drug or an explosive substance may

(f) require that person to remove his/her underclothing.

Since the passing of the Criminal Justice (Forensic Evidence) Act, 1990, certain other powers have been granted in relation to persons held under S.4 and S.30.

For the purpose of forensic testing all or any of the following samples may be taken where a garda not below the rank of superintendent authorises it:

(1) A sample of

(a) blood

(b) pubic hair

(c) urine

(d) saliva

(e) hair other than pubic hair

(f) a nail

(g) any material found under a nail.

(2) A swab from any part of the body other than a body orifice or a genital region.

(3) A swab from a body orifice or a genital region.

(4) A dental impression.

(5) A footprint or similar impression of any part of the person's body other than a part of his hand or mouth.

Before samples specified at 1 *(a), (b), (c), (d),* 3 and 4 above may be taken the appropriate consent must be given in writing.

Samples at 1 *(a), (b)* and 3 may be taken only by a doctor and 4 may be taken only by a doctor or dentist.

Appropriate consent means:

(1) in the case of a person who is seventeen years or over, the consent of that person;

(2) in the case of a person between the ages of fourteen and seventeen, the consent of that person and of a parent or guardian;

(3) in the case of a person under fourteen years, the consent of a parent or guardian.

Where the required appropriate consent is refused without good cause, the court in any subsequent proceedings may draw such inferences as appear proper. This does not, however, mean that a person may be convicted of an offence solely on an inference drawn from such refusal. This does not apply to cases where the person is under fourteen years or where the consent has been refused by a parent or guardian.

Prior to the taking of samples or requesting consent the person must be informed:

(i) of the offence in which it is suspected that s/he has been involved;

(ii) that authorisation has been given to take samples and of the reasons for which it has been given;

(iii) that results of any tests on the samples may be used in court proceedings.

Where consent is required s/he must also be informed of the consequences of refusing such consent.

Conditions of Custody

Reasonable time for rest must be allowed. Meals must be provided: at least two light meals and one main meal in any twenty-four hour period. A person may have meals brought in at his/her own expense where it is practicable for the garda in charge to arrange it. There must be reasonable access to toilet facilities.

If held in a cell, a garda must make half-hourly checks. This should be increased to quarter-hourly checks for a period of two hours or more where the person detained is drunk or drugged. A garda should be accompanied when checking a person of the opposite sex who is alone in a cell. Persons under seventeen should be held in cells only when there is no other secure accommodation available.

Force must not be used against a person in custody unless it is necessary for the purposes of self-defence, preventing escape or injury to himself or others, damage to property or evidence or where it is necessary to secure compliance with lawful directions. Where force is used it must be reported to the superintendent of the district. If the person in custody makes a complaint this fact must be recorded.

Medical treatment must be provided if a person in custody
– is injured;
– is drunk or drugged and unresponsive;
– is unresponsive (not related to alcohol or drugs);
– appears to be suffering from a mental illness;
– requests such attention because of some serious medical condition e.g. heart condition, diabetes, epilepsy, etc. or the garda in charge believes it is necessary because the person has in his/her possession medication for such condition.

If a person in custody asks to be examined by a doctor of his/her choice at his/her own expense the garda in charge shall, if and as soon as practicable, arrange it.

An immediate relative must be informed where the person in custody has been removed to a hospital or other suitable place.

Visits and Communications
By a Solicitor
An arrested person must have reasonable access to a solicitor of his/her choice. The consultation may take place in the sight, but out of hearing, of the gardaí.

By Other Persons
A relative, friend or other person may visit, provided that the garda in charge is satisfied that the visit can be adequately supervised and that it will not hinder or delay the investigation of the offence concerned.

An arrested person may make a telephone call of reasonable duration or write a letter, again provided that the garda in charge is satisfied that it will not hinder the investigation of crime. A garda may listen to the call and read any letter.

Before an arrested person has a supervised visit or communicates with a person other than his/her solicitor, s/he must be informed that anything said during the visit or in the communication may be given in evidence.

Interviews

Before an arrested person is interviewed, the garda conducting it must identify himself/herself and any other garda present by name and rank. Not more than two gardaí may question the detainee at any one time and not more than four gardaí may be present at any one time during the interview.

If an interview has lasted for four hours it must be either terminated or adjourned for a reasonable time.

Interviews should not take place between midnight and 8 a.m. except where:

– the garda in charge has reasonable grounds for believing that a delay in questioning could lead to injury to persons, damage to property, interference with evidence or escape of accomplices;
– the detainee was taken to the station between these hours;
– the detainee is in custody for a serious offence and consents to the interview.

A detainee who is intoxicated (alcohol or drugs) to the degree that s/he is unable to appreciate the significance of the question put must not be questioned unless directed to by the garda in charge who has reasonable grounds for believing that to delay could lead to injury to persons, damage to property, interference with evidence or escape of accomplices.

Persons Under Seventeen Years

A person under seventeen years should not be questioned or asked to sign a statement unless a parent or guardian is present. Exceptions to this are where the garda in charge so directs because for instance

– it has not been possible to inform the parent/guardian;
– the parent/guardian has not attended the station;
– the garda in charge has grounds for believing that to delay questioning the person could involve risk of injury to persons, damage to property, interference with evidence or escape of accomplices;

– the garda in charge has reason to suspect the parent/guardian of complicity in the offence or that his/her presence could result in an obstruction of the course of justice.

Where such exceptions apply, the garda in charge should, unless it is not practicable to do so, arrange for some other adult (not a garda) to be present.

A record must be kept of each interview. This may be written, electronic, etc. It should include details of the time, the interview began and ended, any break in it, the place, the names and rank of the gardaí present and any complaints made by the detainee in relation to his/her treatment.

GARNISHEE

Basically, the term Garnishee means a person who is garnished or *warned* or put on notice. The word is especially applied and used in law to a debtor who is warned by the order of a Court to pay his debt not to his immediate creditor but to a person who has obtained a final judgment against such a creditor. Simply put, 'A' owes 'B' and 'B' owes 'C'. 'C' obtains a final judgment against 'B' and, in turn, gets a court order of garnishee against 'A', obliging 'A' to pay whatever he owes to 'C'. It is a legal device whereby the middle person, 'B', is both owed and owes money.

'C' will initially make an ex parte (one sided) application to the appropriate court. The application is an affidavit (a statement in writing and an oath, and sworn before someone who has authority to administer it). The affidavit must show and exhibit that final judgment has been obtained or received and that the debt is still unsatisfied and to what amount and that another person is indebted to such debtor and is within the jurisdiction. If satisfied, the court will grant a conditional order to permit the garnishee the opportunity to dispute the issue. The conditional order must be served upon the judgment debtor or his solicitor. The judgment debtor may be an individual or a firm. If, after service of the Court Order, the judgment debtor (garnishee) does not appear in court or does not pay into court the amount due, or does not dispute the debt due, then the court may order execution.

To issue execution is to put in force the sentence or order of the law in a final proceeding. If the garnishee should dispute his liability the court, instead of making an order that execution shall issue, may order that any issue or question necessary for determining his liability be tried at law. The person who recovers his debt under the garnishee procedure is also entitled to his costs. In recent times, pension funds, insurance monies and lottery winnings have been the subject of garnishee proceedings.

Finally, the person seeking relief by way of garnishee must have obtained a final judgment against his debtor and be aware that his debtor is owed money.

GUARANTEES

In law, there are many kinds of guarantee. In this article, we shall concentrate on guarantees which concern consumer goods. A guarantee is an undertaking by the manufacturer or retailer to repair or replace faulty goods. A guarantee can also cover the provision of spare parts.

One has to be very careful about the guarantee period because it will last, perhaps, six months or a year from the date of purchase. It is open to the consumer to seek redress under the terms of the guarantee or under the Sale of Goods and Supply of Services Act, 1980. It is extremely important to be aware of the clauses and conditions attached to the guarantee. For example, it may state that unless a fault is reported within a specific period, the guarantee will not be valid; electric kettles, toasters and such like usually have a guarantee card and it is essential that the card be completed and posted back to the manufacturer at or about the time of purchase. If this is not done, the guarantee may fail; even if the guarantee card is not returned it is open to the purchaser to seek redress under the Sale of Goods and Supply of Services Act and it is incumbent upon the supplier to ensure that the goods are satisfactory.

Guarantee cards are very important for anyone who receives a present indirectly as a third party. It will not be open to the third party to seek redress should the goods be unsatisfactory under the Sale of Goods and Supply of Services Act: only the person who actually purchased the goods is protected under the act. However, it is open to the third party to proceed under the guarantee, which is why the guarantee card should be returned promptly.

A final word of advice: where an item fails to work and the buyer feels entitled to redress, do not attempt to repair the item in any way. This may cause more serious damage and invalidate any claim the purchaser may have.

GUARDIANSHIP

Guardianship is the duty to maintain a child and the right to make decisions affecting that child's upbringing e.g. education, religion, adoption, travel abroad, etc. It should not be confused with custody which is the right to physical care and control of a child. Custody is just one aspect of the guardianship relationship.

When a child's parents are legally married to each other they are automatically the joint guardians of their children. If the parents are not married then only the mother has any automatic rights in this respect. The natural father may be appointed joint guardian. Where the mother consents to this and the father's name is on the birth certificate the procedure is quite straight-forward in the District Court. If the mother objects to this then he must apply to the District or Circuit Court and it will decide basing its decision on what it considers to be the best interest of the child. If it is granted to him it is never final: it may be revoked. The only way a mother ceases to be the guardian of her child is by placing that child for adoption. If a child is placed for adoption and the father has been appointed guardian then his consent to the adoption is required.

HABEAS CORPUS

The purpose of a writ of habeas corpus is to command somebody to produce an individual. This writ is of very ancient origin and it takes its name from the two mandatory words *Habeas, Corpus*. This writ is used and an order sought when a person is wrongfully detained. The terms of the order are to produce the person to the court and to show cause as to why he or she is being detained. If the detention is unlawful the court will make an order directing that the person be discharged from whatever custody he or she is in. If the detention is lawful the court will not interfere with the detention. The most frequent use of this device is when a person is wrongfully imprisoned. It may also be used when a person is in military custody or when a person is detained in a mental home incorrectly.

HIRE PURCHASE, DEFERRED PAYMENT AND LEASING

Very simply put, hire purchase is a method of buying goods which involves three parties, namely buyer, seller and hire purchase company. The buyer takes possession of the particular goods or items he wants from the seller. The seller is then paid by the hire purchase company. The buyer, in a number of instalments (weekly, monthly or quarterly), repays the hire purchase company the price of the goods or items plus an interest charge because, in effect, the buyer has received a loan.

The most important legal aspect of a hire purchase agreement or transaction is that the buyer does not become the legal owner of the goods or items until the final instalment is paid. The hire purchase company is still the legal owner and the buyer is regarded in law as the hirer. The Hire Purchase Acts, 1946 and 1960 govern hire purchase agreements or transactions in Ireland. Among some of the rules and regulations laid down by the above two Acts are:

(1) A sale must involve a minimum of five instalments if it is to be regarded as a hire purchase transaction.
(2) A copy of the hire purchase agreement must be forwarded to the buyer within a reasonable time of signing the agreement, for example fourteen days.
(3) The hire purchase agreement must be printed and bear a stamp.
The agreement must show two things:
    (a) the cash price, *and*
    (b) the hire purchase price so that the buyer will be aware of the extra charge he incurs by using the hire purchase system.
(4) If the buyer has paid more than one-third of the hire purchase price, the hire purchase company *must* get a court order before the company can repossess the goods if the buyer (hirer) defaults on the repayments.
(5) When he has paid half the price of the goods the buyer may, if he wishes, return the goods and end the agreement provided the goods are in good condition.

The two acts which govern hire purchase lay down certain implied conditions which are attached to all hire purchase agreements. These implied conditions are:

(1) The buyer (hirer) shall have complete and undisturbed possession of the goods.
(2) The owner has the right to sell the goods when the final instalment has been paid.

(3) The goods must be of merchantable quality, for example they must be fit for the purpose for which they are intended. If the buyer indicates to the seller the reason he is buying the goods and shows that he is relying on the seller's expertise and knowledge that the goods will suit his purpose, then the goods must be suitable for that specific purpose.

The Distinction between Hire Purchase and Deferred Payments

As mentioned already, the buyer in a hire purchase contract is not legally regarded as the owner until the final instalment has been paid. He is the possessor of the goods but not the owner. A *deferred payment* is a credit sale which is similar to a hire purchase agreement in that the buyer pays an initial sum or deposit and pays the remainder of the selling price in instalments. In the deferred payment situation, the buyer becomes the *legal owner* of the goods on the payment of the initial deposit. This is the distinguishing feature between the two systems. In the hire purchase situation, the buyer/hirer has possession and does not become the owner until the last instalment is paid, whereas in the case of deferred payment the buyer becomes the automatic owner at once. If the buyer defaults on the payments in a deferred payment sale, the seller must apply for a court order before the goods can be repossessed. The seller, as already stated, cannot repossess the goods, as in a hire purchase sale, where less than one-third of the price has been paid.

Advantages and Disadvantages

(1) The hire purchase and deferred payment approaches create an increased demand for goods which increases turnover and profits. This is generally good for the economy, especially if the goods are manufactured in Ireland.

(2) The systems enable people to raise their standard of living.

(3) It allows business people and traders to purchase plant and machinery, assets and equipment without having to find the total capital cost of these goods.

(4) It gives financial institutions a profitable outlet for the use of deposits.

As in most things there are some disadvantages:

(1) People may be tempted to buy goods that are not really necessary and, therefore, may end up living beyond their means.

(2) Hire purchase and deferred payment prices are usually considerably greater than the cash price.

(3) The 'true' rate of interest is much greater than the stated nominal rate because interest is calculated on the sum borrowed over the repayment period. For example, the buyer/hirer does not get the benefit of reducing balance interest calculations. A rough rule of thumb is that a nominal rate of 10 per cent in a hire purchase sale works out at a true rate of 19.2 per cent.

(4) The administrative and accounting costs involved are high, which means that their interest rates are high.

(5) Finally, the goods which people buy are often out of date, e.g. computer equipment, or worn out before the loan is repaid. This means that the buyer is still paying for goods from which he is deriving no further benefit.

Leasing

Leasing is a system devised for the *use* of goods, plant or machinery without the user buying the said goods, plant or machinery. Under this system, the owner allows a third party to use the goods in return for rental repayments. It is important to remember that no property in the goods passes, or is ever intended to pass, to the third party, in other words the lessee never becomes the owner. The user has possession but does not and never will have ownership. A leasing agreement can be either short term or long term, financial or operating. In a financial lease the lessor or owner is not responsible for the repair and maintenance of the goods leased. However, in an operating lease the lessor is responsible for the repair and maintenance of the goods. Leasing agreements are subject to the protection of the Sale of Goods and Supply of Services Act, 1980.

HOLIDAYS

Disappointment with holidays gives rise to an incredible degree of dissatisfaction. Every autumn, solicitors' offices fill up with people who feel very disgruntled with the way they have been treated on their holiday. It is an area in which solicitors generally find that their clients' emotions run very, very high.

Essentially, a holiday is governed by the law of contract. A contract arises when a person undertakes to provide a service for another person in consideration of that person paying for that service (*see* page 35). If the person in that situation provides a service and is not paid, he is entitled to sue. On the other hand, if the person pays for the service and the service is not provided that person is entitled to sue. It is rare in these situations that the service is not provided at all; the general complaint concerns the manner in which the service was provided.

There are usually three parties involved in these situations. The *consumer* normally goes to a *travel agent* to book his holiday and comes to an arrangement with the travel agent whereby he is to be provided with a holiday. The travel agent then books the particular holiday through a *tour operator*. So effectively the form of the contract will depend on the tour operator. It will generally be noted in the contract entered into between the consumer and the travel agent that the travel agent will state specifically that he is acting as agent for the tour operator. In this situation a disappointed holiday maker will usually sue the tour operator. It may also be necessary to join both travel agent and tour operator in the proceedings. It is very important to ensure that a tour operator is bonded. One would be entitled to look for evidence of such bonding and not merely to accept a sign on the travel agent or tour operator's window to the effect that he is bonded.

When a holiday maker is disappointed with his holiday, what remedies are available to him? The only real redress is that he can sue for damages. Most of these contracts include a clause whereby all parties agree to submit any dispute arising out of the contract to arbitration. After an arbitrator has made his award, the parties are free to accept it or may appeal an arbitrator's decision to the courts. It should be emphasised that one may only sue arising out of a breach of the particular contract. For example, if you are hit by a car on holiday, you clearly cannot sue the travel agent or tour operator. Also, in the case of an injury arising out of travel on an aeroplane, one only has two years in which to commence a court action against the airline. The most common breaches of these types of contracts relate to the condition of the accommodation, the meals provided and failure to provide flights at the appointed time.

Holidays (Employees) Act, 1973

The purpose of this Act is to provide an allocation to employees for annual leave and to establish certain public holidays.

The Act applies to all employees apart from outworkers, seafarers, certain employees of state bodies, certain agricultural workers and close relatives of the employer maintained by him/her and living in that employer's house or farm.

Annual Leave

There are two methods by which an employee may qualify for annual leave

(a) *Qualifying month basis:* an employee who works 120 hours (110 if under eighteen years) in any month qualifies for one-twelfth of statutory annual entitlement in respect of each such month. Basic entitlement is to three working weeks where there are twelve qualifying months of service.

(b) Where in any leave year an employee works 1,400 hours (1,300 if under eighteen) s/he qualifies for the full statutory entitlement for that year. Therefore, employees who during any given month or months work less than the 120 hours (or 110) can still earn their full quota of leave by working 1,400 hours (1,300 if under eighteen years).

Part-time employees as defined in the Worker Protection (Regular Part-time Employees) Act, 1991 are entitled to six hours for every 100 hours worked and to proportionately less for periods of less than 100 hours. Regular part-time employees are entitled to an unbroken period of annual leave based on

– the leave entitlement earned over the first eight months of the leave year   *or*

– two-thirds of the total leave entitlement earned in the leave year.

Leave is to be taken in the same pattern as their working hours. If an employee works fifteen hours per five day week and three hours per day, annual leave must be based on a three hourly day.

When Can Annual Leave be Taken?

The employer decides on this. However, the employer must consult with the employee or his/her trade union at least one month beforehand. The leave must be given within the relevant leave year or not later than six months afterwards. Failure to give annual leave can result in prosecution.

Any day on which an employee is on certified sick leave cannot be a day of annual leave.

Public Holidays

There are eight:

New Year's Day (1 January)
St Patrick's Day (17 March)
Easter Monday
First Monday in June
First Monday in August

Last Monday in October (Hallowe'en)
Christmas Day (25 December)
St Stephen's Day (26 December).

All full-time employees, all regular part-time employees (as defined by the Worker Protection (Regular Part-time Employees) Act, 1991), part-time and day-to-day employees who have worked 120 hours in the five weeks preceding the public holiday are entitled to all eight public holidays.

There are certain alternatives, at the election of the employer, to taking public holidays on the day in question. These are:
– a paid day off within a month of the holiday
– an extra day's annual leave
– an extra day's pay.

Note that in certain employments covered by Joint Labour Committees the employer's right to decide is limited to some extent; where a public holiday is on a day on which an employee would not have worked for a full day that employee is still entitled to a full day's pay.

HOMICIDE

Homicide means the killing of a human being by a human being. It may be lawful or unlawful. An example of lawful homicide is the execution of an accused sentenced to death by a competent court. Self-defence, accident or misadventure may make a homicide an excusable homicide. Misadventure or accident could arise in a boxing ring where an opponent lands a punch to the head of his opponent and death results. Self-defence may excuse a homicide provided that the force used was proportionate to the attack made.

Unlawful homicide includes the following:
(1) Aggravated Murder (Capital Murder)
(2) Murder
(3) Manslaughter
(4) Concealment of birth
(5) Infanticide
(6) Suicide

Aggravated Murder (Capital Murder)

This classification applies to:
(a) Murder of a garda acting in the course of his/her duty.
(b) Murder of a prison officer acting in the course of his/her duty.

(c) Murder done in the course of certain offences under the Offences Against the State Act, 1939, or in the course of activities of an unlawful organisation. The offences concerned include usurpation of the functions of government, obstruction of government or the President and interference with certain public servants.

(d) Murder in the state for a political motive, of a foreign Head of State, a government member or diplomat of a foreign state.

Where a person (other than a child or young person) is convicted, the penalty is imprisonment for life with the specification that a minimum period of forty years be served. In the case of an attempt to commit such murder, a minimum period of twenty years' imprisonment is the penalty. The powers regarding temporary release and remission for good behaviour are restricted.

Up until the passing of the Criminal Justice Act, 1990, the penalty for treason, capital murder and certain military offences was death by hanging. The distinction between capital murder and 'ordinary' murder and hence the severity of the punishment, was that in capital murder further aggravating circumstances existed such as the occupation of the victim or the activity of the accused when the killing occurred. The 1990 Act abolished capital punishment.

The malice aforethought, or intention for capital murder, now aggravated murder, was debated at length in the case of the *People* v. *Murray* (1977). Basically, the Supreme Court took the view that there must be an intention to kill a garda or prison officer or a diplomat as the case may be, or recklessness that the person to be killed is a member of the garda siochana, etc.

The last execution took place in 1954—the practice since then had been to commute death sentences.

Murder
Murder is the unlawful and intentional killing of another person.

> When a man of sound memory and of the age of discretion unlawfully killeth any reasonable creature *in rerum natura* under the King's peace, with malice aforethought, either expressed by the party or implied by law, so as the party wounded. . . die of the wound. . . within a year and a day after the same.

As can be seen from the above quotation, to get a conviction in a murder case a number of matters must be proved. The person who stands accused must be legally sane. He must be over seven years of age, though in the case a child between seven and fourteen years, 'mischievous discretion' must be proved, that is it must be shown that the child was able to distinguish between right and wrong and that he knew that what he was doing was morally wrong. Knowing that the act was against the law is not enough.

The killing must be unlawful: not all killings are (*see* below). The victim must have been a living person, so an unborn child is not included. The killing must have taken place in peacetime as opposed to during the course of a war. Intention to kill or to cause serious injury must have been present. Finally, the death of the victim must have occurred within a year and a day of the act which it is alleged caused it. The penalty for murder is imprisonment for life.

The word 'unlawfully', in the definition, means without justification or excuse, and malice aforethought is the lawyer's way of describing the intention that is necessary for the act of murder. *Malice* may be expressed or implied. *Express malice* occurs where 'A' says he is going to kill 'B' by shooting him dead and actually does so shoot him. *Implied malice* is that which a court implies from the circumstances surrounding the killing. Death following within a year and a day is a common law rule and it persists today. The purpose of the rule is obvious. A cut-off point has to take place and if the injured person survives beyond the time limit, that is, a year and a day, his death cannot in law be attributable to the original assault so as to constitute murder. The accused, however, may be charged with other offences.

Manslaughter

This is of two kinds:

   (*a*) voluntary or intentional *and*
   (*b*) involuntary or unintentional.

Manslaughter is the unlawful killing of another without malice aforethought. Voluntary manslaughter may happen where one person kills another in a heated manner such as a fight or a remark caused by grave provocation by the deceased. Provocation has been defined as some act done by the deceased to the accused which would cause in a reasonable person a temporary and sudden loss of self-control, rendering him so subject to passion as to make him, for the moment, not master of his mind.

If provocation is pleaded, it is for the trial judge to decide if there is any evidence of provocation and if the trial judge so decides, it is then for the jury to make up its mind that the provocation did or did not exist. It is extremely important to bear in mind that there must be no cooling off period. In other words it would not be open to an accused to plead provocation by saying that he was offended by the words at 9.00 a.m. and at 11.00 a.m. he carried out the act of manslaughter. The effect of provocation is that it may reduce the killing from murder to manslaughter.

An involuntary manslaughter results from an act by a person who did not intend to kill or cause grievous bodily harm but nevertheless intended some degree of harm. A person may commit manslaughter where the act he carries out is lawful but he carries out the act with a huge element of negligence so as to amount to recklessness. The negligence or recklessness must show such disregard for the life and safety of others as to amount to a crime. Judge Davitt, in the case the *People* v. *A.G.*, warned 'there are different degrees of negligence, fraught with different legal consequences'. In the above case, a person was charged with manslaughter arising from the driving of a car. To prove manslaughter, the negligence must be of a very high degree such as to involve the risk of substantial personal injuries to other road users.

Concealment of Birth

This is the offence of secretly concealing the body of a dead child. It is not essential that the child be born alive. What is important, where it is not alive at birth, is whether the child was of sufficient maturity to have been capable of living. Merely abandoning the body is not enough; there must be some attempt to prevent the body being found.

The penalty is two years' imprisonment.

Infanticide

A woman will be guilty of infanticide if:
  (*a*) by an act or omission she causes the death of her child (under 12 months)
  (*b*) in circumstances that amount to murder *but*
  (*c*) at the time of the act or omission, the balance of her mind was disturbed by reason of her not having fully recovered from the effects of giving birth.

Infanticide is treated as manslaughter by a court when it is deciding on the penalty to be imposed.

Suicide

This is the crime of self-murder. It is an offence unlawfully and intentionally to take a human life, even if that life is one's own. In Ireland in 1991 there were 311 suicides reported. As a coroner's report is not allowed, by law, to state that death resulted from suicide it is accepted that the actual figure may be much higher. A 1992 Bill viewing suicide as a social disease rather than criminal behaviour proposes to remove it from the area of criminal law.

An attempt at suicide is an offence and a person charged may be tried in the District Court. A person who persuades another to commit suicide is guilty of murder as is a person who survives a suicide pact.

IDENTIFICATION PARADES

Where a suspect agrees to go on an identification parade or, indeed, asks to be placed on one, that parade should be conducted along the following lines:

(1) The suspect should be placed among a number of other persons (at least eight) who are, as far as practicable, of similar height, age, general appearance, dress and position in life. If there are two suspects they may be put on a single parade with at least twelve volunteers. However, if they have quite different appearances separate parades should be held.

(2) The suspect may take up any position s/he wishes in the parade and, after a witness has left, change his position if he wishes before the next witness is called.

(3) The suspect may have a solicitor or friend present at the parade. Where a solicitor is asked to attend, s/he should ensure that it is carried out fairly and should note the type of place in which it is being carried out, the appearance and dress of the suspect and the volunteers and any other relevant matters which may be of use later.

(4) Other than the suspect(s), the volunteers, the conducting officer, the officer in charge of the investigation of the case and the suspect's friend or solicitor, no other person should be present at the parade.

(5) When the line up is formed, witnesses should be brought in one by one. The conducting officer should say to each witness
    This is an identification parade. I want you to look very

carefully at this line of men/women and see if you can identify the person (who assaulted you or who was on the . . . day of . . . etc.). Do not say anything until I ask you a question. When a witness has studied the line up s/he should be asked whether or not s/he can identify anyone.

(6) A witness may ask to see a person walk, to hear him speak or to put on or take off an item of clothing.

(7) Where a witness indicates that he has made an identification, he should usually be asked to touch that person on the shoulder. However, an identification can be made by pointing at or describing the person in question.

(8) When the parade ends, a suspect should be asked if s/he has any complaints about the manner in which it was carried out.

(9) The person conducting the parade must keep a record of the proceedings.

Informal Identification

Where a parade is not possible, the gardaí may resort to a more informal procedure. This often occurs where a garda is approached in a street and informed of an incident by a victim or a witness to it. In such cases the garda may go with this person in the hope of finding the culprit. This type of identification procedure should take place in situations where there are reasonable numbers of persons present, e.g. cinema, court room, etc. The less conspicuous the subject is the greater the value of the identification.

In trials where the verdict depends substantially on visual identification of the accused, the jury should be informed in general terms of the fact that in a number of cases visual identification has been discovered subsequently to have been erroneous.

INJUNCTIONS

Circumstances may arise where the payment of substantial damages will not be adequate to meet the wrong done. In other words, immediate relief is what is sought and what will help the offended party; the law has devised the injunction to give this relief. An injunction may be defined as an order of a court, requiring a party either to do a specific act or to refrain from doing a specific act. If the court requires a party to do a specific act, that is called a mandatory or positive injunction and, likewise, if it requires a party to refrain from doing a specific act, that is called a prohibitory or negative injunction. The essence of the remedy is that it prevents repetition or continuance of the offending act.

Injunctions may be further classified according to the period of time for which the order of the court is to remain in force. A perpetual injunction is final and is usually granted after a full hearing. However, before the perpetual is granted, the offended party may have sought what is called an interlocutory injunction, which is a provisional measure taken at an earlier stage in the proceedings. It is usual for such an order to continue in force until the trial of the action or further order. Occasionally applicants seek what is called an interim injunction and this is still more temporary than the interlocutory and remains in force only until a named day, for example 1 January at 10.00 a.m., or so soon thereafter as counsel may be heard.

Some commentators would suggest that there is no substantial difference between an interim injunction and an interlocutory injunction. It can happen that an injunction may be granted even though the applicants' legal rights have not as yet been infringed. This is called a quia timet injunction, because the applicant fears that a wrong will be done to him if the order of the court is not made. Once the court grants an injunction, or an undertaking is given, it remains in force and must be obeyed until it is discharged by the court.

It is important to remember that an injunction is not a cause of action like a tort, which is a civil wrong, but a remedy like damages. Before a court grants an injunction, whether interim, interlocutory or perpetual, it will take into account the balance of convenience. This would seem to be the guiding light where injunctions are granted. It is what is called a discretionary remedy, that is it may be granted or it may not, depending on the circumstances of the case. The following are some of the purposes for which an injunction may be granted:

(1) to restrain trespass to land by persons or structures;
(2) to compel removal of overhanging structures;
(3) to restrain trespass by a hunt;
(4) to restrain nuisance by noise pollution, vibration, smells;
(5) to bar a respondent from his home;
(6) to compel a landlord to allow peaceful re-entry;
(7) to restrain a trade union from expelling its members;
(8) to restrain passing off;

(9) to stop infringement of a patent;

(10) to prevent a trustee from permitting a breach of trust;

(11) to prevent the removal of a child from Ireland and to take that child to a foreign country.

As mentioned earlier, the granting of an injunction is at the discretion of the court. Factors which may be taken into account are the plaintiff/applicant's behaviour: 'He who comes to equity must come with clean hands.' This basically means that the person seeking the assistance of the court, by way and in the form of injunction, must in fact be truthful to the court. It is unlikely that the court would grant an injunction against a person of unsound mind who would be incapable of understanding the nature of the relief granted, or against a minor, if there are no effective means of enforcing the order.

If *acquiescence* or *laches* enters the picture, it is unlikely that an injunction will be granted. Acquiescence means that if a person having a right and seeing another person infringing it, stands idly by so as to give the impression that he consents to it being infringed, he cannot afterwards complain of the infringement. Laches is an unreasonable delay by the plaintiff after the infringement of his right such as to make the granting of an injunction unjust to the defendant/respondent. The term 'laches' involves two elements: the delay and the consequent injustice.

Developments in this area have resulted in two injunctions, one called a Mareva injunction and the other an Anton Peiller injunction. Basically, the Mareva injunction allows a plaintiff who can show that he is entitled to money from a defendant, and that there is a risk that the defendant will remove assets from the jurisdiction or dispose of them so as to make them unavailable, to restrain the defendant from disposing of the assets or removing them from the jurisdiction.

The Anton Peiller order or injunction is a mandatory injunction requiring the defendant to permit the plaintiff to enter his premises and remove property; the fear is that the property may be disposed of or destroyed by the defendant before the application is heard. This development was brought about by the appearance of 'pirates', that is, those who make unauthorised copies of copyright recordings, and 'bootleggers' who made unauthorised recordings of live performances. Recordings incorrectly obtained would, of course, be disposed of or destroyed, therefore defeating the applicant's case. However, by granting what is virtually a search warrant, the applicant can search for the unauthorised copies of copyright recordings and unauthorised recordings of live performances.

One word of caution to the person who may seek an injunction. It is essential that all applications be accompanied by an undertaking as to damages. This means that if at the trial of the action the applicant who got either the interim or interlocutory injunction and is now refused a perpetual injunction he will be obliged to compensate the defendant for his losses. A simple example: if a person living next to a green where it is proposed to hold a circus for a week or fortnight seeks an injunction he or she will be obliged to give an undertaking as to damages. If the person is successful in getting the interim or interlocutory injunction, and it turns out at the hearing of the action that he or she was not entitled to such an order, the damages could be considerable. Loss of revenue for a fortnight from a circus could, in fact, be substantial.

INSURANCE

How often has one heard the sentence, 'If only I was insured, I would not be in the difficulty and predicament that I am now in.'

The importance of being insured cannot be over-emphasised. Individuals and businesses have collapsed because they were not insured and they had to make available their personal property and interests to satisfy claims made as a result of not being insured. Even if there is no risk of litigation, it is wise to be insured so that, in the event of illness or incapacity, the person may be in receipt of a regular payment to exist.

A contract of insurance may be defined as a contract where one person, called the insurer, undertakes in return for an agreed premium to pay to another person, called the insured, a sum of money on the happening of a specified event. It is important that the specified event must have some element of uncertainty about it. The uncertainty may be either

(1) in the case of life assurance *or*
(2) in the fact that the happening of the event depends upon accidental causes.

In (1) above, that is life assurance, we know that death will come to all but what is not known is the time of its happening, therefore there is uncertainty. In the case of number (2), the happening of the event depends upon accidental causes and the event, therefore, may never happen at all. It is, therefore, called an accident. It is not uncommon for people to insure against accidents. One other thing about the event that is specified in the policy/insurance is that it must be of a nature that results in actual loss to the insured. Examples include marine insurance, in which the sum insured becomes payable on the happening of an accident at sea; fire insurance, in which the sum becomes payable on the happening of a fire; life insurance, in which the sum insured becomes payable on the death of the insured and accident insurance, in which the sum insured becomes payable on the happening of any other event.

The law does not lay down any particular form, but contracts of insurance are usually in writing. In practice, the contract embodies what is called a policy which states all the terms of the contract. The person seeking insurance is obliged to fill in what is called a proposal form. The completed proposal form is then forwarded to the insurers who examine the risk that is sought to be insured against. It is a fundamental principle of insurance law that the utmost good faith must be observed by each party. Special facts may be known only to the person seeking insurance, so disclosure of these special facts must be made to the insurance company so that they can assess the risk they are being asked to bear. The concealment of any fact may result in the policy being voided, in other words set aside; the insurance company will not pay out on the policy.

Therefore, it should be a contract of the utmost good faith—*uberrima fides*. The Supreme Court, in a recent judgment, ruled that, in order to set aside a policy of insurance, the task of proving that the insured knew the true condition rested with the insurance company and that it was not sufficient to prove that the insured ought to have known the true position. It is acknowledged that not many people seeking insurance read the actual written contract that is presented to them for signature. However, if a difficulty arises concerning any clause or provision of the contract it will be construed against the insurance company drawing up the actual written contract. This is known as the *contra proferentum* rule. The court may take the view that the insurance company is in the stronger position and to balance the situation that if a clause of condition is challenged and if a construction can be put in favour of the insured that such a construction will be so put. The arrival of over the phone or over the counter insurance has given the courts the opportunity to rule on the disclosure factor or, indeed, on a non-disclosure factor.

If a policy of insurance is concluded over the counter or over the telephone and no questions are asked, it is not open, generally speaking, to the insurance company to repudiate the contract of insurance on the grounds that certain disclosures were not made to the insurance company. This interpretation of the non-disclosure rule puts the onus back on the insurance company to ask the appropriate questions.

The individual who wishes to have immediate insurance while the proposal form is being considered may be given temporary cover by the issue of what is called a cover note. This is, in effect, a separate contract and will contain such terms as are appropriate to such a short-term contract. It may be given for a week or a month or a quarter to allow the insurance company to assess the risk they are asked to insure against. At the end of the cover note period, the insurance company may refuse to accept the risk and it is open then to the individual to seek insurance elsewhere.

When the event that is insured against occurs, for example in a motor policy, it is usual for the insured to have to fill out an accident report form. This may have to be done within a specified time and if a notice is not given in accordance with the policy the insurer could repudiate liability. It is not unusual in some motor insurance policies to find a clause which insists that the motor propelled vehicle be kept and maintained to a certain standard. If an accident occurred and if an engineer establishes that the clause or condition was not adhered to, it is open to the insurance company to seek to repudiate the contract of insurance. Factors that ought to be seriously considered when entering into insurance policies is the duration of the policy and its renewal date. The construction of the terms and clauses of a policy of insurance is a question for the court to decide. The size of print in insurance policies is immaterial. The following is a list of rules which has evolved over the years to assist in the construction of a policy of insurance:

(1) The intention of the parties must prevail.
(2) The whole of the policy must be looked at: it is not sufficient to look at the introduction or the middle portion of it or its conclusion.
(3) The written words will be given more effect than the printed words.

(4) The policy must be construed in accordance with the ordinary laws of grammar.

(5) The ordinary meaning of the words will be adapted.

(6) In the case of ambiguity, the *contra proferentum* rule will be applied.

(7) An express term in the policy of insurance overrides any implied term.

These are just some of the rules that are used by the courts to establish the nature of the policy. It is essential for the insured person to read the print, whether big or small, so that he or she knows how the risk is, in fact, insured.

When disaster occurs, most people who have insurance believe that the insurance company will foot the entire bill. But this is not necessarily so. A high percentage of risks, for that is what they are, are either under insured, insured on the wrong basis or not insured at all. Insurance companies often use what is known as the rule of average. This means that if you insure your dwelling house for £100,000, when it should be insured for £200,000, and part of it burns down causing damage of £25,000, the insurance company will only pay out £12,500. Their argument is that the insured is under insured by 50 per cent and, therefore, they are only liable for 50 per cent of the damage.

There are a number of areas that affect small companies, for example buildings, stock, plant machinery, consequential loss, employer's liability, public liability and, finally, product liability. The biggest mistake people make is to insure buildings or premises at the market value of the building. What they should actually consider doing is to insure the building for the cost of completely re-building the property, since the market value may be considerably more or less than the rebuilding cost depending on location.

Where insurance for stock is concerned, it is essential that companies keep proper accounts. If stock is damaged, the insurance loss adjuster will visit the premises to assess a claim for damage to stock. He will often ask to see the last set of accounts. Unless the company can show that the stock was on the premises at the time of the loss, its claim may not be met in full, even if it has sufficient cover. Premiums are only high when the risk is high and individuals can do a great deal to reduce risks and, hence, premiums. Installing anti-theft devices and burglar alarms will reduce premiums, as will the introduction of sprinkler systems.

JURY SERVICE

It is a jury's task to enquire on a matter of fact and declare the truth upon such evidence as is before them. Many readers may recollect the memorable film, *Twelve Angry Men*, where Henry Fonda, by his eloquence and determination in the jury room, changed the intended verdict of 'guilty' to that of 'not guilty'.

The provisions of the Juries Act, 1927 were successfully challenged in the celebrated case of *De Burca* v. *Attorney-General* (1976). The Act excluded from jury service all citizens who were without a minimum ration qualification in respect of a house or land, and exempted women from service subject to an individual woman's right to apply to serve. In the Supreme Court decision in the De Burca case, it was laid down that the jury must be drawn from a pool broadly representative of the community so that its verdict would be stamped with the fairness and acceptability of a genuinely diffused community decision.

Qualification for Jury Service

A person is qualified and liable for jury service if he or she is a citizen whose name is entered in the register of Dáil electors and is not less than eighteen years of age nor more than seventy years of age and is not ineligible or disqualified.

Persons ineligible include the President of Ireland, the Attorney-General and members of his staff, the Director of Public Prosecutions and members of his staff, barristers and solicitors actually practising as such, members of the garda síochána, prison officers and members of the Defence Forces. Persons who are disqualified include those who have been sentenced to imprisonment or penal servitude for life or for a term of five years or more or to detention under Section 103 of the Children Act, 1908. Some persons may be excused as of right: members of either House of the Oireachtas, members of the Council of State, a person in holy orders, medical practitioners, dentists, nurses, midwives; these lists are not exhaustive and the appropriate forms should be examined to see who is ineligible, disqualified or excused as of right. The jury system is one of the cornerstones of our legal system and it is essential that it continue to play its role in the administration of justice.

LARCENY

Larceny is defined as the taking, without the right to and without the owner's consent, of anything which is capable of being stolen, with the intention of permanently depriving the owner of that thing. If something has value and belongs to another it is capable of being stolen.

Accepting the change from a £20 note in a shop when only £10 was handed over and not pointing out the mistake is an example of larceny. Attempting to steal is also a crime.

The penalties vary, depending on the type of crime. However, there is a standard ten-year jail sentence in cases where no other special punishment is provided.

Burglary

This is entering a building as a trespasser with the intention to steal, attempt to steal, cause grievous bodily harm, rape a woman or unlawfully damage the building.

The maximum penalty on indictment is imprisonment for fourteen years.

Smashing a window and snatching goods from inside is a burglary.

Aggravated Burglary

A burglary with a difference! This is committed where a burglar is armed, at the time of the burglary, with a firearm, imitation firearm, air-gun, offensive weapon or explosive. Offensive weapon, in this case, means any article made or adapted to cause injury or incapacitation; this might be a broken bottle, a cosh or piece of cloth made into a gag.

The penalty on indictment is imprisonment for life.

Car Theft

Car/motorbike theft carries a penalty of £1,000 and/or twelve months' (summary) or on indictment £2,000 and/or five years' imprisonment.

Having implements to be used in the theft of a car/motorbike carries a penalty of five years' penal servitude and/or a fine.

Where a firearm or imitation firearm is carried the penalty is higher e.g. up to fourteen years' imprisonment.

Embezzlement

An employee who steals goods or money from his/her employer commits the offence of embezzlement. The difference between embezzlement and larceny is that, in embezzlement, the property is taken before it comes into the possession of the employer, whereas in larceny the property is taken after it has come into the possession of the employer. Embezzlement is diverting!

Fraudulent Conversion

This occurs where a person is entrusted with the property of another and converts it, or the proceeds of it, to his/her use or to the use or benefit of another. A director who uses company money for his/her own use or a solicitor who keeps a house deposit instead of passing it on to the seller of the property are examples.

The penalty is ten years' imprisonment and/or a fine.

Handling

A person who handles stolen property, otherwise than in the course of a theft, knowing or believing the property was stolen or thinking such property was probably stolen is guilty of an offence.

Handling includes receiving, helping to remove, storing, keeping possession of, etc. or arranging to do any of these things.

The maximum penalty is fourteen years' imprisonment and/or a fine.

In relation to such offences as embezzlement, blackmail, demands with menaces, obtaining property by false pretences, etc., for which the penalty is ten years' imprisonment and/or a fine, the penalty for a related handling offence is also ten years.

Possessing Articles with Intent

Possessing articles made or adapted for use in a larceny, burglary, car theft, a demand with menaces, etc., carries a penalty of five years' penal servitude and/or a fine.

Robbery

Robbery is the offence of stealing from another using force or threatened force. Wrenching a shopping bag from the owner's hand is an example.

An attempt to rob, i.e. an assault with intent to rob, is also an offence.

The maximum penalty on indictment is imprisonment for life. However, this type of case may be tried in the District Court unless the value of the property involved is over £200, in which case the consent of the DPP is necessary.

Pickpocketing

The maximum penalty is ten years' imprisonment and/or a fine.

MAINTENANCE

There is a legal obligation on spouses to maintain each other and their children (if any). If one spouse fails in this duty the other spouse may go to court to sue for maintenance. If a successful maintenance order is granted, obliging the errant spouse to pay periodical sums i.e. weekly, monthly, etc., for the maintenance of the applicant and dependent children. Dependent children are those under sixteen years or in full-time education up to twenty-one years or who are handicapped.

Most applications for maintenance are dealt with in the District Courts; the High Court has the power to hear applications but the procedure is more complicated and difficult.

In the District Court the application is made by first taking out a summons. A date is then set for the case to be heard, usually from between six to eight weeks. The award of maintenance may be up to £100 per week for the spouse and £30 per week for each child. Appeals can be taken to the Circuit Court.

The procedure is more complicated in the Circuit Court and legal advice is therefore advisable. There is also a greater time lapse between the time of application and the date of hearing. A Circuit Court can award any amount of maintenance; there is no ceiling. Appeals can be taken to the High Court.

A maintenance order is never final; applications may be made to have it varied at any time when, for example, circumstances change through redundancy, unemployment, etc.

If a spouse fails to comply with a maintenance order you may :

(1) Apply for an Attachment of Earnings order, whereby certain sums will be deducted from the spouse's income by his/her employer. Obviously this is only applicable in cases where the spouse is an employee (District Court).

(2) Have a warrant issued for the spouse's arrest. Penalties are imprisonment for up to three months and goods may be sold to provide for the amount of the arrears (District Court).

(3) Have the Circuit Court try the spouse for contempt. If successful the spouse may be sent to jail until s/he complies with the order.

Judicial Separation and Maintenance

In cases where a judicial separation is being sought in the Circuit or High Court, special provisions in relation to maintenance apply, e.g. periodical payments, lump sums, etc.

Maintenance and the Family Outside Marriage

There is no legal obligation on couples living together outside marriage to maintain each other. However, since the passing of The Status of Children Act, 1987 a parent, generally the mother, of a child born outside marriage can apply for maintenance for that child against the father in the same way as a married woman may apply for maintenance from her husband.

Maintenance proceedings are held 'in camera' (in private). Maintenance payments are not tax deductable.

MARRIAGE

A marriage is a contract which leads to a change in the legal status of the persons entering it. Like all contracts, there are certain conditions which must be met before it can be deemed valid. It is, with very few exceptions, a lifelong contract and thus not to be entered lightly.

Since 1975, the minimum legal age for marriage is sixteen years. In exceptional cases the High Court may grant exemptions. There would need to be serious reasons for such exemptions to be granted. Prior to 1975 the minimum legal age was fourteen years for a boy and twelve years for a girl.

The parties to a marriage must be single. If at the time of the marriage ceremony either party is already validly married to a third party, the marriage is void and the crime of bigamy is committed.

A person who has already entered a marriage contract cannot validly marry again until the first spouse dies or the first marriage is terminated by a valid foreign divorce. A Catholic Church annulment does not alter the legal status of the parties; they are still married in the eyes of the state.

The other main conditions are that there must be consent to the marriage by both parties, one party must be male and the other female, they must not be closely related, and, the laws of the place where the marriage is to be celebrated must be observed. In many countries the civil and religious aspects of a marriage are dealt with separately. A civil ceremony takes place before a state official in perhaps a town hall and later, if desired, the couple celebrate the marriage in a church ceremony. In Ireland it is possible to have a civil ceremony only, in a registry office, or to have a church ceremony where the clergyman acts both for the church and the state. If couples plan to travel abroad to marry it is essential that they observe local laws. There have been problems in the past, in particular in relation to marriages celebrated in Lourdes which were later found to be invalid under Irish law, as at the time they were solemnised local French law had not been observed: the Church weddings had not been preceded by civil ceremonies.

Being married carries certain rights and duties:
- the right to each other's company, that is to live together as husband and wife.
- the right to joint and equal guardianship of their children and the duty to maintain them and rear them with due regard to their physical, social, and moral welfare.
- the duty to maintain each other.
- the right to part of each other's estate; a spouse cannot be excluded in a will though, of course, this right may be waived.
- the right to apply for a protection order or a barring order if in a violent relationship.
- the right to be consulted and to have one's consent required in writing before the family home is sold. It should be noted that this of itself does not confer any automatic rights to part of the proceeds of that sale.
- the constitution in Article 41.3 provides that the state pledges itself to guard with special care the institution of marriage on which the family is founded and to protect it against attack.
- the state recognises marital privacy. It was the recognition of this right that was partly responsible for the de-criminalising of contraception in 1972.
- married couples have the right to adopt children.

MATERNITY (PROTECTION OF EMPLOYEES) ACT, 1981

This Act provides for the right of female employees to take unpaid time off from work during certain specified periods both before and after birth. It must be noted that the exercise of this right is subject to certain stringent requirements.

The Act applies to all female employees in insurable employment (earning £25 or more per week) including part-time employees who are normally expected to work at least eight hours per week and have thirteen weeks continuous service. It does not apply to women who work under fixed term contracts of less than twenty-six weeks or under fixed term contracts of which there are less than twenty-six weeks to run.

Notification to Employer
A woman wishing to take maternity leave must notify her employ-

er in writing at least four weeks before the leave is due to start. She must also supply a medical certificate stating the expected date of birth. If additional leave is to be taken (four weeks) then the employer must be notified in writing at least four weeks before the end of the maternity leave period. The rules in relation to notification are strict and failure to comply with them can result in a woman losing her entitlement.

Time Off for Medical Checks
A woman is entitled to time off for ante-natal and/or post-natal care and for other medical appointments. An employer should be notified of the date and time of the appointment not later than two weeks before the date of the appointment; in certain cases submitting for the employer's inspection the relevant appointment card.

Maternity Leave
The Act provides for fourteen consecutive weeks leave. It is up to the woman to decide when it is taken provided that at least four weeks are taken before the expected date of the birth and at least four weeks are taken after the birth. An additional period of four weeks leave may be taken immediately following the maternity leave period.

Right to Return to Work
A woman is entitled to return to work provided that she notifies her employer in writing at least four weeks before she is due to return. She should state the date she intends to return on. It has been held in the High Court that failure to give this notification is a fair reason for dismissal.

Sometimes it is not 'reasonably practicable' for an employer to take a woman back into the exact job she had prior to her maternity leave. In such a case an employer may offer 'suitable alternative employment' under a new contract of employment. The terms and conditions, however, must not be 'substantially less favourable to her' than previously.

Maternity Pay
The Act does not make provision for 'maternity pay' as such, so maternity leave is 'unpaid' in the strict sense. However, under the Social Welfare Acts, a woman on maternity leave is entitled to social welfare payments at the rate of 70 per cent of the woman's

reckonable earnings provided she is qualified. No social welfare benefit is payable during a period of additional maternity leave. For those women who are actually paid, while on maternity leave, by their employers the additional four week period of leave is unpaid.

MINIMUM NOTICE AND TERMS OF EMPLOYMENT ACTS, 1973 TO 1991

These Acts require that minimum periods of notice be given by employers and employees when terminating contracts of employment and that written terms of employment be given to employees.

Who is Covered?
All employers.
All employees except
   (1) employees employed for less than eight hours a week with the employer concerned.
   (2) Gardaí and Defence Forces.
   (3) Civil servants.
   (4) Employer's immediate family who work and reside with him/her in the same house or farm.

Notice to Employees
An employer who wishes to dismiss an employee who has been in his/her continuous employment for thirteen weeks or more must give that employee a minimum period of notice. The required period depends on the employee's length of service

13 weeks' − 2 years' service	1 week
2 years' − 5 years'	2 weeks
5 years' − 10 years'	4 weeks
10 years' − 15 years'	6 weeks
15 years' +	8 weeks.

An employee may agree to waive his/her right to notice and accept payment in lieu.

Notice to Employers
An employer is entitled to at least one week's notice from an employee who has been in his/her continuous employment for thirteen weeks or more.

Terms of Employment

An employer is obliged to supply employees with a written statement of the terms and conditions of employment. It should include:

- the commencement date;
- details of pay, overtime, bonuses;
- whether pay is to be weekly or otherwise;
- holiday entitlements;
- sick pay schemes and pension arrangements;
- details of hours of work, overtime, etc.

Disputes about matters covered by the Act should be referred to the Employment Appeals Tribunal.

MISUSE OF DRUGS ACTS, 1977, 1984 AND REGULATIONS

The law on the misuse of drugs is concerned with the misuse of controlled or harmful drugs. A controlled drug is one which is specified in the legislation (there are 125) or one which is declared to be controlled by order of the government. These drugs include cannabis, cannabis resin, cocaine, mescaline, morphine, pethadine, opium and heroin. The main offences under the legislation are possession and possession for unlawful sale or supply but included also are importation, cultivation, forging of prescriptions and many more.

If a garda, with reasonable cause, suspects that a person possesses a controlled drug unlawfully he may without a warrant:

(1) search that person, detain him for that purpose and, where necessary, require him to go to a garda station to be searched;

(2) search any vehicle and, if necessary for that search, require it to be taken to a specified place;

(3) examine, seize and detain anything found which might be required as evidence.

Generally, if a search of a premises is to take place a warrant is required.

Arrest

If a garda, with reasonable cause, suspects that a person has in his possession a controlled drug for the purpose of selling it or supplying it to another, unlawfully, he may arrest that person without a warrant. Generally, the quantity that the person possesses deter-

mines whether it was for supply or not. Other matters such as
whether the person was a drug user or not would also be of rele-
vance. Apart from this provision, before a garda may arrest without a warrant, he must with reasonable cause suspect that the person has committed an offence or attempted to and that:
 (*i*)   he will abscond if not arrested;
 (*ii*) the garda has reasonable doubts as to the person's identity
       or abode;
 (*iii*) the garda knows that the person does not live in the state or
       has doubts as to whether the person so resides.

Penalties
The penalties for *possession* differentiate between cannabis and all
other drugs. Where the *cannabis* is for personal use, the penalties
are, in the case of a first offence, on summary conviction a maximum fine of £300; on an indictment a maximum fine of £500; for
a second offence a maximum fine of £400 or £1,000 respectively
and for a third offence a fine of £1,000 and/or twelve months'
imprisonment or, on indictment, an appropriate fine and/or
three years' imprisonment.
   In *any other case* the penalties are on summary conviction a
£1,000 fine and/or twelve months' imprisonment or an appropriate fine and/or seven years' imprisonment on conviction on
indictment.
   The penalties for *possession for the purpose of unlawful sale* or *supply* are on summary conviction a £1,000 fine and/or twelve
months' imprisonment or on conviction on indictment to an
appropriate fine or to imprisonment for life or such lesser period
as the court decides or to both a fine and imprisonment. The
court also has the power in many situations to request medical
and welfare reports on the convicted person, such reports to
include recommendation as to medical treatment.
   Other offences dealt with in the legislation include cultivating
the opium poppy or cannabis plant; forging or altering prescriptions; printing, publishing or distributing pro-drug literature;
importing and exporting controlled drugs, etc.

NEGLIGENCE
Negligence has been defined as omitting to do something which
a prudent and reasonable man would do, or doing something

which a prudent and reasonable man would not do. Some legal commentators give two meanings to negligence. One is that it may be a method of committing other torts, that is civil wrongs such as trespass, defamation, nuisance; the other that it is an independent tort or civil wrong in its own right. Whichever view the reader takes, it is regularly pleaded by plaintiffs in actions against defendants.

A plaintiff who alleges negligence must prove a number of essentials:

(*i*)   that the defendant owed the plaintiff a legal duty of care;
(*ii*) that the defendant broke his legal duty of care; and
(*iii*) that the plaintiff suffered damage in consequence of the breach, and that the damage must not be too remote.

As regards number (iii), there must be a sufficiently close connection between the conduct and the resulting injury to the plaintiff.

The Duty of Care

Whether a duty of care is owed in any given circumstances is a question of law to be decided by the judge. It has been said that a person 'is entitled to be as negligent as he pleases towards the whole world if he owes no duty to them'. If a duty of care is owed, the next question to be addressed is, to whom is the duty of care owed? Lord Atkin's celebrated leading judgment in *Donoghue* v. *Stevenson* (1922) (the snail in the ginger beer bottle) established the general rule that the duty of care is owed to one's 'neighbour'.

His Lordship took the view that 'you must take reasonable care to avoid acts or omissions which you can reasonably foresee would be likely to injure your neighbour'. Atkin, in his judgment, asked the rhetorical question 'who then in law is my neighbour?', to which he gave the answer, 'persons who are so closely and directly affected by my act that I ought reasonably to have them in contemplation as being so affected when I am directing my mind to the acts or omissions which are caused in question'. It will be noted from the answer given by Atkin to his own question that he lays emphasis on acts and omissions.

Contributory Negligence

In many instances which cause loss, one party will be completely without fault and the other party entirely at fault. But what happens when both parties, by their negligence, contribute to the loss?

By virtue of the Civil Liability Act, 1961 where one party con-
tributes to his own loss, that party may still recover compensation.
However, the amount recoverable will be reduced by the contri-
bution which the court views as having been caused by the plaintiff alleging loss.

Liability may attach to the following: employers, occupiers,
suppliers of goods, carriers and those in the transport business,
highway users. A word about each in turn.

An employer owes a duty of care towards his employee. The
standard of care is that of a prudent employer who would not
expose a worker to unnecessary risks. The employer is under an
obligation to provide a safe place of work, proper equipment and
sufficient training to produce competent staff. Should injury or
loss be sustained by an employee, the circumstances of the case
will be examined. If it is established that the employer failed to
provide competent staff or a safe place of work or, indeed, a safe
system of work, he may be held responsible for the injury or loss
sustained by the employee.

In occupiers' liability the occupier is held responsible for
injuries caused to those who enter his property. People may come
onto premises in one of three ways; the court may take the view
that a person is an invitee or a licensee or a trespasser. An invitee
comes onto the property on business in which the occupier has
an interest; it is the occupier's duty to prevent injury from unusual dangers of which he knew or ought to have known. Examples
of unusual dangers include: a dark stairway or one without a
handrail, a greasy hotel floor, a spillage of cooking oil on a shop
floor. A licensee is an entrant permitted on the premises for his
or her own benefit. Examples of licensees are: entrants to public
parks, to museums, forests and, indeed, visits to hospitals. The
duty of an occupier in this instance is to warn the entrant of any
concealed dangers of which the occupier has knowledge.

What may not be a danger to a grown person may be a concealed danger for a person of tender years. In *Rooney* v. *Connolly*
(1986), a young girl went to her local church to light a candle at a
shrine. The only place vacant for her to light a candle was in the
middle row. In attempting to light the candle, the sleeve of her
blouse caught fire and she was badly burnt. The Supreme Court
took the view that the candle holder was a concealed danger, having regard to the child's tender years and that the occupier of the
church, namely the priest, had a duty not to expose her without
warning to a danger of which he actually knew.

Not only is it necessary for a supplier of goods to take reasonable care that those goods are in reasonable condition, the controller of goods and the repairer of goods is under a duty to make sure that nothing happens that will cause injury or damage to the consumer. Carriers and transporters of passengers and goods are obliged to take reasonable care in the performance of their duties. Matters of which carriers have to be mindful are the maintenance of the vehicle, its operation and the entering and leaving of the vehicle by fare-paying passengers. Many injuries have been sustained by passengers when trains or buses move off too quickly after passengers have entered. Reasonable time ought to be given to the passenger to reach either a safety rail or a seat.

Finally, those who use the highway must take reasonable care not to cause injury or damage to other highway users. Numerous court cases have arisen over the negligent use of motor vehicles.

NEIGHBOURS

The recent court case involving a husband and wife who planted trees on a bog of which they are the registered owners, shows how differences of opinion between neighbours can end up in court and how people can be jailed for not obeying a court order. The couple planted trees on the bog using proceeds of a lotto win but local people who claimed rights to cut turf on the bog objected. They secured a court injunction stopping the couple from further planting. This was ignored. The couple were jailed until they agreed to come back to court and purge their contempt.

When unhappy differences arise, the judges hearing the cases are mindful of the short-term and long-term implications of their judgments and attempt to soothe feelings by suggesting that the differences be ironed out between the conflicting neighbours. Adjournments are often granted to facilitate this. It is not always an option to move house so that for peace of mind it is essential that sense, patience and understanding prevail to resolve the dispute.

Lord Atkin in *Donoghue* v. *Stevenson* (1932) stated 'the rule that you are to love your neighbour becomes, in law, you must not injure your neighbour and the lawyer's question, "who is my neighbour?", receives a restricted reply. You must take reasonable care to avoid acts or omissions which you can reasonably foresee would be liable to injure your neighbour. Who then, in law is my neighbour? The answer seems to be persons who are so closely and directly affected by my act that I ought reasonably to have them in contemplation as being so affected when I am directing my mind to the acts or omissions which are called in question.'

The above extract is quoted to show that one's neighbour can be injured by *acts or omissions*. This extract has been the subject of exhaustive analysis and examination but for the purpose of this article we emphasise that acts and omissions can cause unhappy differences to arise between neighbours.

At the onset, an attempt should be made to resolve the dispute by dialogue and, if this fails, perhaps the services and assistance of an independent third party should be sought. However, introducing a third party requires the agreement and commitment of the disputants and if this avenue of approach fails the only course left may be litigation (court action). The disputes and unhappy differences can be many and varied and only a few can be noted here:

(1) Tree roots growing under neighbouring land.
(2) Overhanging branches growing over neighbouring land.
(3) Smoke.
(4) Destructive animals.
(5) Unreasonable noise.
(6) Unreasonable vibration.
(7) Dust.
(8) Fumes.
(9) Massage Parlours.
(10) Sewage.
(11) Blasting.

The list is well nigh inexhaustible.

Nuisance, in law, consists substantially of the unreasonable interference with another person in the exercise of his/her rights. The above list is capable of adjustment and enlargement. The heightened concern with the environment has made the public more sensitive to acts and omissions, of individuals, companies and governments alike.

Sometimes, distressingly, a dispute ends up as a breach of the peace. Arising from this, a summons may be served upon the offending party and a court appearance will follow. This is where the judge has to do a balancing act; attempt to prevent further breaches of the peace, punish the wrongdoer and try to effect a reconciliation between the disputing parties. Occasionally orders are made that are not carried out and contempt proceedings may issue, thus exacerbating the matter and often resulting in the differences lasting a very long time. Memories are long in Ireland!

A person's home is often viewed as his castle but the law expects the owner to be reasonable about the activities that he carries out there. Likewise, it is not enough for a person to say that he may do what he likes. There is a threshold beyond which the next door neighbour can object and request an abatement of the offending nuisance. The neighbour who alleges nuisance must prove nuisance and, to be successful in court, it is essential to be able to show that there was actual damage caused to your property or that there was an interference with your enjoyment of your property and the interference was caused by the acts or omissions of your next door neighbour.

The above list of nuisances, if clearly proven, may result in damages being awarded. Occasionally damages may not be adequate. It may be necessary to seek an injunction to prevent the continuation of the nuisance. In seeking an injunction it is necessary to give an undertaking as to damages and this, when fully explained by a solicitor to the client, may result in a different approach. The undertaking as to damages could be enormous and, consequently, the implications of litigation should be seriously considered before embarking upon it. This means that if the applicant fails to get his permanent injunction, he will be obliged to pay the damages and costs of the other side.

NUISANCE

Nuisances are of two kinds: public nuisance and private nuisance.

Public Nuisance

This is some unlawful act or omission which endangers or interferes with the comfort, safety or lives of the public generally, or some section of the public. It is a public nuisance to keep a brothel, to block the public highway, and to erect a factory which emits smoke, fumes or dirt so as to cause inconvenience or discomfort, and possible illness, to persons in the area. A public nuisance is a crime and action may be taken by the Attorney-General on behalf of the public, who may sue also for an injunction to stop further offences. Furthermore, it is open to a private person to sue the person committing the public nuisance if he, the private person, can show that he has suffered peculiar damage over and above that suffered by the public generally. For example, to dig a hole in a public highway without authority is a public nuisance and a crime. If a citizen falls into the hole, or if the hole interferes with the citizen's right of way into his own home, he may show peculiar damage to himself and sue the person or the persons who excavated the hole.

In *Boyd* v. *GNR*, a doctor on his rounds was held at a level crossing for a very considerable time. He sued the railway company and was successful. He was able to show that he had suffered damage over and above that suffered by the public generally.

Private Nuisance

This is an unlawful interference with a person's use of his property or with his convenience, comfort or health. Generally speaking, there are two main types of private nuisance: interference with the enjoyment of land (in its broadest sense) generally; and injuries to servitudes. Servitudes or easements are rights of way, rights of light and rights of support of land. Of these two types the first is the more important.

Noise, fumes, vibrations, smells, dirt, smoke are acts which may constitute nuisance. Nuisance is not actionable *per se*. It is necessary to establish that some damage has occurred to the owner of the land to enable him to sue successfully. The basic rule is that land should be used so that it will cause no harm to another. This broadly means 'live and let live': one should be reasonable in one's acts or omissions in regard to neighbours (*see* page 125).

A balance has to be maintained between the right of the occupier to do what he likes with his own property and the right of a neighbour not to be interfered with. It is impossible to give any precise formula, but it may broadly be said that a useful test is, perhaps, what is reasonable according to the ordinary uses of mankind living in society. Relevant factors include health and comfort, standard of comfort and the use of the nuisance. Under health and comfort and standard of comfort, the rule of thumb seems to be the ordinary comfort of life and the fact that it may vary from locality to locality. There is a difference between O'Connell Street on a Saturday night and a residential area. The only exception under this head seems to be that an interference with light to a building will be dealt with equally, whether it occurs in one area or another, for one requires the same light to sew everywhere. A person cannot take advantage of a heightened personal sensitivity. One must be reasonable in the circumstances and there must be 'give and take'.

The allegation that the trade or occupation or industry is for the public benefit is no defence in law. In the case *Bellew* v. *Cement Ltd*, the fact that the cement company provided the building industry with most of its cement was not a defence to its creating noise, fumes and dust. Mr Bellew, the owner and occupier of lands adjacent to Cement Ltd's premises, was successful in his action. The occupier of property is the proper person to bring the action and the person who creates the nuisance is the proper person to be sued.

The following defences are good in cases of nuisance: authority, triviality, lawful use of the land and reasonableness. It is a defence to show that a statute allows the act or omission in question. The person who it is alleged created the nuisance may prove that the act or omission is small and trivial. For example, a once-off fire in the garden where the owner burns leaves may not constitute a nuisance, for the law does not concern itself with trifles. Minimum discomfort must be expected on the basis of give and take.

The Distinction between Trespass and Nuisance

Trespass	*Nuisance*
1. Actionable *per se*.	1. Must prove damage.
2. Direct physical interference to land (e.g. placing rubbish on a neighbour's land).	2. Need not be direct (e.g. allowing bricks from a ruinous chimney to fall on a neighbour's land).
3. Wrongful entry of an object or person on another's land.	3. No entry necessary. Can be created on defendant's own land.
4. May consist of one act only.	4. Usually more than one act is necessary.
5. Trespass to land is not a crime.	5. Public nuisance is a crime.

OFFENSIVE WEAPONS

These include firearms, knives, flick knives and articles made or adapted to cause injury or incapacitation. The definition is quite broad.

The main offences relating to offensive weapons include the following:

Having, without good reason, in a public place, a knife or any other article which has a blade or which is sharply pointed is an offence for which the maximum penalty is £1,000 and/or twelve months' imprisonment. Carrying such an article for the purpose of self-defence would not constitute a good reason, whereas a recreational or occupational purpose would.

Having a flick knife in a public place without good reason or having any other article made or adapted for use for causing injury to or incapacitating a person is a more serious offence. The maximum penalty in this case is a fine and/or five years' imprisonment. 'Any other article' includes a firearm, a cosh, CS gas, a club, etc.

Where a person while committing an offence or during a fight produces, in a way likely to intimidate another person, any article capable of inflicting serious injury, the maximum penalty is a fine and/or five years' imprisonment.

A trespasser armed with an offensive weapon is liable to a maximum penalty of a fine and/or five years' imprisonment.

See FIREARMS, LARCENY

PARTNERSHIP

A partnership which requires a minimum of two persons is defined as 'the relation which subsists between persons carrying on business in common with a view to a profit'. The Partnership Act, 1890 defines business as including 'every trade, occupation or profession'. The Limited Partnership Act of 1907 stated that the maximum number of partners that may exist in a venture is twenty for an ordinary business and ten for a banking partnership. In most situations the partners to a venture will have come together and have a Partnership Agreement drawn up between them setting out their mutual obligations and benefits as part of an implied contract. The 1890 Act gives guidelines for determining whether or not a partnership exists in Section 2(3) which states 'The receipt by a person of a share of the profits for business is prima facie evidence that he/she is a partner in that business but does not of itself make him a partner.'

In relation to the management of a partnership Section 5 of the 1890 Act should be noted in that it says 'Every partner is an agent of the firm and his other partners for the purpose of the business of the partnership; and the acts of every partner who does any act for carrying on in the usual way business of the kind carried on by the firm of which he is a member bind the firm and his partners, unless the partners so acting has in fact no authority to act for the firm in the particular matter, and the person with whom he is dealing either knows that he has no authority, or does not know or believe him to be a partner.' As will be seen, even though a partner's authority to bind the firm may be very restricted, his firm will still be bound by his acts if they are done within the apparent scope of his authority. In relation to the liabilities of partners, each partner will have to contribute equally to the losses of a partnership, unless there is an agreement to the contrary. What this effectively means is that if the partnership owes money to a third party the third party can sue any individual partner for the entire amount. Such a partner who was sued would obviously have a right of indemnity against the other partners. A partnership would normally come to an end by agreement or as provided for in the partnership agreement. It will also usually be ended by the bankruptcy or death of a partner. If the partnership is wound up its assets are sold, debts paid and any money left over distributed among the partners.

PATERNITY

Paternity in its ordinary meaning is that some man is the father of a child. This would appear to be self-evident. However, there are cases where a woman may have more than one sexual partner and in these situations it is not always easy to know who the correct father is. There is provision under Section 38 of the Status of Children Act, 1987 to seek the court's direction and to have blood tests taken. This matter mostly raises its head in relation to maintenance proceedings in the District Court where the respondent is denying that he is the father of the child for whose benefit the maintenance is sought. The rules relating to these procedures are quite complicated and are contained in the Blood Testing (Parentage) Regulations, 1988 (S.I. No. 215 of 1988). A court may draw an inference from a person's failure to comply with a direction for blood testing, as appears proper in the circumstances.

PRIVACY

In Ireland, the judges have developed a constitutional right to privacy in certain areas. There does not seem to be a general 'right to privacy'. If there is an interference with one's right to privacy, it is open to the person to seek a remedy in tort, which is a civil wrong. It is not necessary to deal, in this article, with trespass to land, goods, the person or nuisance - we deal with these in the appropriate places.

In *McGee* v. *A-G,* the Supreme Court recognised that married couples have a constitutional right to marital privacy which basically entitles them to have access to contraceptives.

In the celebrated case of *Kennedy & Arnold* v. *Ireland,* the President of the High Court held that the tapping by the state of the plaintiffs' telephones infringed a right to privacy and awarded the plaintiffs damages totalling £50,000. It was contended that the normal precautions and procedures operated by Ministers for Justice had not been adhered to in relation to the tapping of the plaintiffs' telephones.

If phone tapping is to take place, it must be for the investigation of serious criminal or subversive activity which cannot be investigated by any other means. The judge refused to accept that the warrants ordering the phone tapping were improper. He took the view that they were illegal and, consequently, that the constitutional right to privacy of the plaintiffs was violated. In his judgment he said 'The right to privacy includes the right to privacy in respect of telephonic conversations and the right to hold such conversations without deliberate, conscious and unjustified interference with, and intrusion thereon by servants of the state who listened to such conversations, recorded them, transcribed them and made the transcriptions thereof available to other persons.' However, the judge held that interference with telephonic conversations could be justified where the 'exigencies of the common good' required such interference.

PROBATION

Probation is granted where a court believes that it is inexpedient to inflict any punishment other than a nominal one. The court may dismiss a charge or make an order discharging an offender conditionally on his/her entering into a bond with or without sureties, to be of good behaviour and to appear for sentence when called on during such period, not exceeding three years, as may be specified in the order.

The offender may be placed under the supervision of a probation officer and may have other conditions imposed, e.g. regarding residence or abstention from alcohol.

There are a number of offences for which a probation order cannot be granted, e.g. failing to provide breath/blood samples on being detained for alleged drunk driving.

REDUNDANCY PAYMENTS ACTS, 1967-91

Redundancy Payments Act, 1967
Redundancy Payments Act, 1971
Redundancy Payments Act, 1973
Redundancy Payments Act, 1979
Redundancy Payments Act, 1991

Scope

The Redundancy Payments Acts, 1967–91 provide for the making by employers of payments to employees in respect of redundancy, establish a redundancy fund and require employers to pay contributions towards that fund. The Acts also provide for payments to be made out of that fund to employers and employees.

Persons Covered

(1) To be covered, an employee must be in employment which is insurable for all benefits under the Social Welfare Acts, or to have been in such employment in the four years prior to the redundancy.

(2) S/he must be aged between sixteen and sixty-six years.

(3) S/he must be normally expected to work for eight hours or more per week for the same employer. S.8.2. Worker Protection (Regular Part-time Employees) Act, 1991.

(4) S/he must have been continuously employed for 104 weeks, between the ages of sixteen and sixty-six years.

(5) By Section 4(3) of the 1967 Act, persons employed as domestic servants and agricultural workers are covered by the scheme other than
Where the employer is the father, mother, grandfather, grandmother, stepfather, stepmother, son, daughter, grandson, granddaughter, stepson, stepdaughter, brother, sister, half-brother, or half-sister of the employee, where the employee is a member of the employer's household and the employment is related to a private dwelling-house or a farm in or on which both the employer and the employee reside.

(6) Seafarers are covered, unlike in the Minimum Notice and Terms of Employment Act, 1973 and the Protection of Employment Act, 1977.

Employee's Right to Redundancy Payment

An employee covered by the Acts is entitled to a redundancy payment if:

(i) he is dismissed by his employer by reason of redundancy or

(ii) is laid off or kept on short time for a minimum period (four consecutive weeks or for six out of thirteen consecutive weeks).

Definition of Dismissal

Under Section 9 of the 1967 Act, for the purposes of the Acts an employee shall be taken to be dismissed by his employer 'if but only if':

(a) the employer terminates the contract under which he is employed, whether by or without notice, *or*

(b) where under his contract he is employed for a fixed term and that term expires without being renewed under the same or a similar contract (e.g. where a five-year term comes to an end), *or*

(c) the employee terminates the contract in circumstances where he is entitled to by reason of the employer's conduct (S.9(1)), except because of a lock-out by his employer (S.9(5)).

Apprentices

If an apprentice (employed under an apprenticeship agreement) is dismissed within one month following the completion of his apprenticeship, he is not entitled to a redundancy payment. If he is dismissed during his apprenticeship, he is so entitled provided he has fulfilled the service requirements. Employers should ensure that the requisite notice expires during the one month period.

No Dismissal by Employer
Re-engagement by Same Employer

An employee shall not be taken to be dismissed by his employer if his contract of employment is renewed or he is re-engaged by the same employer under a new contract of employment and:

the renewed contract or the new contract is exactly the same as the previous contract and takes effect immediately; or the renewal or re-engagement follows an offer in writing made by his employer before the ending of his employment under his previous contract. This offer should take effect immediately (as above) or after not more than four weeks. Continuity is maintained during this period.

In the above circumstances the employee is not entitled to a redundancy payment.

Section 9(2) of 1967 Act.

Re-engagement by Different Employer

An employee is not deemed dismissed and thus is not entitled to a redundancy payment if:

he is re-engaged by a new employer immediately, on the termination of his previous employment; *or*

the re-engagement takes place with the agreement of the employee, the previous employer and the new employer; *or*

before the commencement of the period of employment with the new employer the employee receives a statement in writing on behalf of the previous employer which:

– sets out the terms and conditions of the employee's contract of employment with the new employer

– specifies that the previous service is continuous

– contains particulars of the previous service, e.g. dates

– the employee notifies the new employer in writing that he accepts this statement.

Section 9(3) of the 1967 Act and Section 19 of the 1971 Act.

Disentitlement to Lump Sum Payment

Refusal to Accept Alternative Employment

You will not be entitled to a redundancy payment if:

(i) your employer has offered to renew your contract or to re-engage you under the same terms and conditions; *or*

(ii) the renewal or re-engagement takes effect on or before the termination of your old contract; *or*

(iii) you have unreasonably refused the offer; *or*

(iv) you have received your notice of redundancy (RPI) and in the two weeks ending the date of dismissal:

  (a) your employer has offered in writing to renew your contract or to re-engage you under a new contract under different terms or conditions;

  (b) the offer constitutes a suitable offer of employment and would take effect within four weeks of the date of termination of the 'old' contract, *and*

  (c) you have reasonably refused the offer.

Section 15 of the 1967 Act and Section 11 of the 1971 Act.

An employee shall not be entitled to a redundancy lump sum if, being otherwise entitled, such employee is in fact dismissed by reason of misconduct.

Misconduct does not include an employee participating in a strike after the date of receipt of the redundancy notice.
Section 14 of the 1967 Act.

Redundancy Definition

An employee is dismissed by reason of redundancy if his dismissal results from any of the following circumstances:

- his employer has ceased, or intends to cease, to carry on the business for the purposes of which the employee was employed, or has ceased or intends to cease to carry on that business in the place where the employee was so employed, *or*
- the requirements of that business for the employee to carry out work of a particular kind in the place where he was so employed have ceased or diminished or are expected to cease or diminish, *or*
- his employer has decided to carry on the business with fewer or no employees, whether by requiring the work for which the employee had been employed (or had been doing before his dismissal) to be done by other employees or otherwise, *or*
- his employer has decided that the work for which the employee had been employed (or had been doing before his dismissal) should henceforward be done in a different manner for which the employee is not sufficiently qualified or trained, *or*
- his employer has decided that the work for which the employee had been employed (or had been doing before his dismissal) should henceforth be done by a person who is also capable of doing other work for which the employee is not sufficiently qualified or trained.

In determining whether an employer has decided to carry on a business with fewer or no employees, account is not taken of certain members of the employer's family, specifically: father, mother, stepfather, stepmother, son, daughter, adopted child, grandson, granddaughter, stepson, stepdaughter, brother, sister, half-brother, half-sister.
Section 7 of the 1967 Act and
Section 4 of the 1971 Act.

In *Gargan* v. *Hanly* (589/1974), it was held that an offer of employment of similar kind sixteen miles further away did not disentitle an employee when refusing such an offer from a redundancy lump sum on the basis that the new employment 'would have caused a radical change in the conditions'.

Presumptions
In application to the Employment Appeals Tribunal under the Redundancy Payments Acts, Section 10 of the 1971 Act provides for two presumptions:
  (1) that, until the contrary is proved, the employment was continuous;
  (2) that, until the contrary is proved, the dismissal was by reason of redundancy.

Continuous Service
Schedule 3 of the 1967 Act, as amended, defines reckonable service. Employment is taken to be continuous unless terminated by dismissal, or the employee voluntarily resigning his employment. Continuity is not broken by:
  – sickness or injury for a period of not more than seventy-eight consecutive weeks, lay-off, holidays, or any other reason which has been authorised by the employer for not more than twenty-six weeks;
  – service in the Reserve Defence Force;
  – absence from work because of a lock-out by his employer or for participation in a strike;
  – dismissal due to redundancy before attaining 104 weeks' continuous service and resumption of employment with the same employer within twenty-six weeks of dismissal;
  – transfer of a business: the period of employment with the old employer is deemed continuous with the period of employment with the new employer;
  – maternity leave, additional maternity leave or time-off under the Maternity (Protection of Employees) Act, 1981;
  – re-instatement or re-engagement under the Unfair Dismissals Act, 1977;
  – the fact that an employer has not given the required notice under the Minimum Notice and Terms of Employment Act, 1973 or contractual notice, whichever is applicable.

Reckonable Service
Reckonable service is also defined under Schedule 3 of the 1967 Act, as amended, and must be computed to calculate the redundancy lump sum.

Reckonable service excludes absence due to lay off or a strike in the business or industry in which the employee is employed after the commencement of the 1967 Act (1 January 1968).

Reckonable Service includes:

- all or part of a week when an employee is at work or was absent by reason of sickness, holidays or other arrangement with his employer during a period of continuous employment;
- up to fifty-two consecutive weeks' absence due to an occupational injury or disease as defined by the Social Welfare (Occupational Injuries) Act, 1966;
- up to twenty-six consecutive weeks due to illness;
- authorised absence of thirteen weeks in a period of fifty-two weeks;
- absence from work due to strike in the business or industry in which the employee is concerned prior to the commencement of the 1967 Act;
- absence due to lock-out;
- absence due to a strike or lock-out in any other business or industry before the commencement of the Act;
- absence while on maternity leave, extended maternity leave or time off under the Maternity (Protection of Employees) Act, 1981.

For the purposes of the Redundancy Payments Act 'lock-out' means 'the closing of a place of employment or the suspension of work, or the refusal by an employer to continue to employ any number of persons employed by him in consequence of a dispute, done with a view to compelling those persons, or to aid another employer in compelling persons employed by him, to accept terms or conditions of or affecting employment' (Section 6, 1967 Act: *see* Section 9(5), 1967 Act).

'Strike' means 'the cessation of work by a body of persons employed acting in combination, or a concerted refusal or a refusal under a common understanding of any number of persons employed to continue to work for an employer in consequence of a dispute, done as a means of compelling their employer or any person or body of persons employed, or to aid their employees in compelling their employer or any person or body of persons employed, to accept or not to accept terms or conditions of or affecting employment' (Section 6, 1967 Act). Secondary and sympathetic strikes are therefore included but only so long as they relate to terms and conditions of or affecting the employment.

Rights to Redundancy Payment by reason of lay-off or short time

Lay-off

Where an employee's employment ceases because his employer is unable to provide the work for which the employee was employed to do, this cessation of employment will be regarded as lay-off if:

(a) the employer reasonably believes that such cessation will not be permanent *and*

(b) the employer gives notice to that effect to the employee beforehand (S.11(1)).

Short time

Where the employer gives his employee less work to do and either that employee's remuneration for any week is less than one-half of his normal weekly remuneration or his reduced hours of work for any week are less than one-half of his normal weekly hours, he shall be taken to be on short time for that week (S.11(3)).

If an employee has been laid off or kept on short time for four or more consecutive weeks, or within a period of thirteen weeks, for a series of six or more weeks of which not more than three were consecutive, he may be entitled to a redundancy payment. To claim such payment he must give his employer notice of intention to claim redundancy payment in respect of the lay-off or short time, after the expiry of either period and not later than four weeks after the cessation of the lay-off or short time. Alternatively, the employee may terminate his contract of employment by giving his employer notice, which will be deemed to be a notice of intention to claim a redundancy payment as of the date on which such notice is actually given.

Counter Notice by Employer

The employer can still contest any liability to make a redundancy payment. If, when the claim for redundancy payment is made, it is reasonably expected that the employee might enter upon a period of employment of not less than thirteen weeks, the employer can contest the claim. A counter-claim notice must then be served on the employee within seven days. However, the employer's counter-claim will automatically fail if:

(a) the employee continues to be employed by the same employers during the four weeks from the date of the original claim;

(b) the employee has been laid off or kept on short time for each of these weeks.

Redundancy and Employer's Insolvency Fund

This fund (formerly known as the Redundancy Fund) was established under the 1967 Act. Employer PRSI (redundancy) contributions are paid into it and employer rebates are paid from it. Redundancy lump sum payments may be made to employees from the fund under certain circumstances.

Redundancy Procedure

An employer who proposes to dismiss an employee must give the employee notice in writing of the proposed dismissal not less than two weeks before the operative date. A copy must be sent to the Minister for Labour at Davitt House, Dublin. An employer who fails to comply with such provision shall be liable, on summary conviction, to a fine not exceeding £50.

This provision is complied with by handing the employee a completed form RPI. The RPI Form must be given to an employee who has more than 104 weeks' continuous service.

The notice to be given to the employee shall be the greater of the following:

(1) Two weeks' notice under the Redundancy Payments Act.
(2) Notice in accordance with the Minimum Notice and Terms of Employment Act, 1973, which can range from two weeks, in the case of redundancy, to eight weeks.
(3) Notice in accordance with the Contract of Employment.

On the date of dismissal, the employer must give the employee the completed redundancy certificate (RP2), together with the lump sum payment. The employee signs the RP2 in receipt for the payment. It is important accurately to calculate reckonable service in accordance with the rules prescribed in order to complete the RP2.

Failure by an employer to give a redundancy certificate (RP2) or furnishing on it false information is an offence, attracting, on summary conviction, a fine not exceeding £300.

An employee who is entitled to a redundancy payment arising from a claim because of lay-off or short time must also be given a redundancy certificate by his employer. In this case the employer must give the certificate not later than seven days after the service of the notice of intention to claim (by the employee) (S.18).

Extra Money

The Acts do not exclude the possibility of privately agreed redundancy schemes. Employers and employees can agree that payments in excess of statutory ones shall be made, but the employer will not be able to claim a rebate from the Redundancy Fund for the excess payment.

Early Termination

When an employer gives notice to an employee to terminate his contract of employment but the employee wishes to leave before the notice expires, he may give notice *in writing* to his employer to terminate his contract on an earlier date than the date on which the employer's notice is due to expire (S.10(1)).

If the employer has given notice over and above the obligatory period, whichever is applicable, and if the employee's notice of intention to terminate his employment is not within that period, then the employee will lose his right to redundancy payment.

Unless the employer objects, the employee is taken to be dismissed by his employer, and the date of dismissal will be the date on which the employee's notice expires, i.e. the earlier date, and he is therefore eligible for redundancy payment (S.10(2)). If the employer, before the employee's notice is due to expire, gives him notice *in writing* (*a*) requiring him to withdraw his notice and to continue in employment until the date on which the employer's notice expires and (*b*) stating that unless he does so, the employer will contest any liability to pay him a redundancy payment, but the employee unreasonably refuses to comply with the requirements of that notice, then the employee will not be entitled to a redundancy payment by virtue of Section 10(2). (S.10(3))

Lump Sum Payment

When an employee has been dismissed by reason of redundancy (or has terminated his contract as a result of lay-off or short time) he is entitled to a statutory lump sum payment equal to:

- a half week's normal weekly remuneration for each year of continuous and reckonable service between sixteen and forty-one years, *or*
- a week's normal weekly remuneration for each year of continuous and reckonable service between forty-one and sixty-six years, *and*
- the equivalent of one week's normal weekly remuneration.

Such payment is subject to the statutory ceiling of £13,000 p.a. or £250 per week. This ceiling is adjusted from time to time by Ministerial Order.

Calculation of Statutory Lump Sum Payment

The Acts specify the following method of calculation:

- In order to ascertain the number of years reckonable service, the number of weeks in continuous service should be divided by 52. Weeks not allowable as reckonable service are disregarded.
- If the result of the above division produces a remainder of twenty-six or more weeks, that remainder shall be counted as a year of continuous employment. However, if the remainder is less than twenty-six weeks, that period of service is disregarded.
- When the total number of years of continuous employment has to be calculated for service prior to and after the forty-first birthday, any remaining parts of a year in such periods of employment shall be aggregated. The number of full years represented by this aggregate (which must be calculated as outlined above) shall be added to the period of service which the employee attained before his forty-first birthday.

Employer's Claim for Rebate from the Redundancy Fund

The Minister for Labour may make a payment to an employer from the Redundancy Fund amounting to 60 per cent of the statutory lump sum paid to an employee.

However, if an employer fails to comply with the notice provisions the Minister may, at his discretion, reduce the amount of the rebate payable in respect of such lump sum paid to that employee to 40 per cent of the statutory redundancy payment.

The claim form, known as an RP3, must be sent to the Minister within six months of the date of payment of the redundancy lump sum. It shall be accompanied by a copy of the RP2.

The RP3 shall contain certification that the employee:

- ceased employment on the date stated on the RP2, *and*
- the employee received statutory lump sums in accordance with the Acts, enclosing a copy of RP2 signed by the employee.

The RP3 must be signed and dated by the employer.

RESTRICTIVE COVENANTS

Most land when it is sold is made expressly subject to all kinds of restrictions as to its use. Therefore, restrictive covenants are agreements restricting the use of land which are enforceable between the original parties and those who succeed those parties.

A restrictive covenant may be enforced by applying the principles of equity, that is, that a person who acquires property with knowledge that some other person has rights in relation to it will, in conscience, have to observe these rights. An example helps to make this clear: *Tulk* v. *Moxhay* (1848). Tulk sold the central part of Leicester Square to Elms. Elms contracted or covenanted on behalf of himself and his successors not to build on the land. The land was later sold to one Moxhay who knew of this contract or covenant but nevertheless decided to build on the land. What Moxhay did was challenged and the court held that Moxhay was bound by the covenant, that is, not to build. It would be wrong that Elms, who gave a small price for the land, because of the restrictions or the restrictive covenants, should be able to sell it for a larger price free from these restrictions. The case demonstrates that not only was Tulk bound by covenant, but that his successors in title were, and among his successors were Elms and Moxhay. The court intervened to make sure that the restrictive covenants were adhered to.

Most urban land in Ireland is held on very complicated titles. These have resulted from centuries of resettlements and subdivisions. The result of all of these confiscations and resettlements is that a great amount of urban land, owned by one group of people, is subject to rights owned by other people.

Dwellings are subject to restrictive covenants prohibiting the use of the property for certain purposes. For example, use of the property for the sale of intoxicating liquor or as a fish and chip shop may not be permitted. If an attempt is made to use it for either of the above examples, it will be open to the successor in title to enforce the restrictive covenant.

Some other restrictive covenants might be in the form of easements, that is, rights of way or rights to light, which would affect or be affected if the owner of the dwelling house converted his house into a hotel. Restrictive covenants concern land law and land law is, therefore, concerned with a huge variety of rights and interests which may exist in the land and with the various methods of dealing with them. In conclusion, when purchasing land, it is vitally important that proper searches be made so as to establish what restrictions and easements run with the land, because such restrictive covenants and easements can be both a benefit and a blessing and on occasions, indeed, a burden.

SAFETY AT WORK

In 1991, seventy-three people died in work-related accidents while thousands of others were off work for various periods of time. On average there are around 45,000 accidents per year, of which 100 are fatal. Agriculture has the worst record in respect of fatalities, accounting for around fifty deaths per year; in 1991, the actual figure was thirty-five and some of those killed were children. The cost, needless to say, is enormous both in human misery and in monetary terms.

The most common cause of accidents as opposed to deaths in the workplace is the mishandling of goods. This accounts for between 30 and 40 per cent of the total. At the other end of the scale in 1991 were accidents involving electricity of which there were six.

A new approach to safety in the workplace was adopted with the introduction of the Safety, Health and Welfare at Work Act, 1989. It has brought fundamental changes to the whole area of protective legislation. The Act is proactive rather than reactive, encouraging preventative safety measures rather than waiting until the damage is done. All persons at work in all types of employment are protected whereas before this Act only 20 per cent of the workforce was provided for by the existing safety legislation.

Safety, Health and Welfare at Work Act, 1989

This Act provides protection for all persons at work in all types of employment, whether employers, employees or self-employed. Its purpose is to prevent accidents and ill-health in the workplace. Duties are placed on management, employees and others to achieve this end. These duties are set out in Part II of the Act under the following headings.

General duties of:
(i)   employers to their employees;
(ii)   employers and self-employed to persons other than their employees;
(iii) persons concerned with places of work to persons other than their employees;
(iv)   employees;
(v)   designers, manufacturers, etc. as regards articles and substances for use at work;
(vi)   persons who design or construct places of work.

Key Provisions

(i) Duties of employers are to protect the health, safety and welfare of employees. This includes providing and maintaining safe places of work, safe plant and equipment and safe systems of work. They are obliged to provide such information, training and supervision as is necessary to ensure their safety and health. Every employer must consult his employees so as to make arrangements for a safe workplace. Employees have the right to select Safety Representatives to represent them in consultations with their employer. The employer is also obliged to prepare a written safety statement identifying hazards, assessing risks and setting out the arrangements made for dealing with these matters. It is worth noting that a good safety statement is a record of a company's commitment to the set purpose of the Act; a poor one could indicate negligence.

(ii) Employers must also safeguard persons who are not their employees such as contractors, the general public or others who could be affected by their work activities.

(iii) Landlords and occupiers of buildings, or those who have control of buildings must ensure, so far as is reasonably practicable, the safety and health of contractors, the employees of another person, etc. in respect of the place of work, access to and egress from that place and any articles or substances in the place of work.

(iv) Employees must take reasonable care for their own safety and welfare and that of any other persons who may be affected by their work activities. They must co-operate with their employers and others in meeting the requirements of the Act. Where equipment, clothing or other means are provided for securing safety, they must also be used. Defects in the place or system of work which might endanger safety, health or welfare must be reported to management once employees become aware of them.

(v) Designers, suppliers, manufacturers, etc. are required to ensure that all articles or substances for use at work are safe when properly used. Articles here means machinery, equipment, plant, etc. for use in the workplace.

(vi) Designers and builders are obliged to ensure, so far as is reasonably practicable, that the place of work is safe.

The penalty for most offences is £1,000 on conviction in a summary trial. For serious cases on indictment in the Circuit or

Central Criminal Court, there is no limit on the fine and in some cases a term of imprisonment for up to two years may be imposed, or both.

SEPARATION

When a marriage breaks down and a couple decide to separate, the main legal options are
- a separation agreement
- judicial separation.

Separation Agreement
Because this is by way of agreement it is therefore less painful and less expensive. The couple who are separating come to an arrangement the terms of which are then set down in a legally binding agreement. It is usually drafted by a solicitor and signed by both partners. Each partner should have separate legal advice. There is no need to go to court.

Issues which need to be addressed in any agreement should include the following:
- custody of and access to children;
- maintenance;
- provisions regarding the family home;
- the right to inherit part of each other's property—this is usually relinquished;
- expenses resulting from the breakdown;
- taxation;
- the right to live separate and distinct lives;
- a non-molestation clause.

When the agreement has been finalised it may be made a rule of court, by the parties simply making an application to the court. The consequences of breaking such an agreement could then involve one in contempt proceedings.

The effect of a legal separation is to free the couple from the obligation to live together. It does not give the right to re-marry.

Judicial Separation
In a situation of marital breakdown, where a couple cannot agree as to how they should separate, or indeed where one partner is reluctant to separate, a legal remedy may be found in a judicial separation. One spouse applies to the court seeking a decree of separation from the other. A spouse may apply for a decree on the following grounds:

(1) Actual separation for a continuous period of at least three years up to the time of application. In this situation the fact that the other spouse does not consent is not a factor.

(2) Adultery. Proof of some sort is required. If, however, you continue to live with your spouse for more than a year afterwards, then that act of adultery cannot be used as a reason for seeking a judicial separation.

(3) Bad behaviour on the part of one spouse which makes it unreasonable for the other spouse to continue living with him/her. Bad behaviour includes failing to maintain a spouse and children, staying out all night, physical and mental cruelty.

(4) Desertion for a continuous period of at least a year up to the time of application. Desertion means that the departing spouse has no intention of returning. The decision to desert must not be mutually agreed or collusive and the deserting spouse must not have had good reason to depart.

There is a form of desertion called constructive desertion which must be considered. This covers a situation where one spouse has to leave the home because of the other spouse's misbehaviour e.g. violence. Constructive desertion is desertion for the purposes of judicial separation.

(5) Actual separation for a continuous period of at least one year up to the time of application where both spouses agree to the decree being given.

(6) Where the marriage has broken down to the extent that there has not been a normal marital relationship for at least one year up to the time of applying for the judicial separation.

When a court grants a judicial separation, it may make additional orders concerning the following matters:

– family home/farm;
– proper provision for the couple's children (if any) in relation to maintenance, custody, access;
– maintenance of spouse;
– inheritance rights.

Applications for this form of relief may be made in the Circuit Court. There is an obligation on solicitors acting for either side to first discuss with a couple possible reconciliation, mediation services, counselling or the negotiation of a separation agreement without recourse to the courts.

Mediation

Mediation is a service which may be availed of by couples intending to separate and who wish to negotiate between themselves all the terms of their separation. They are helped through this process by an impartial and trained person called a mediator. When agreement is reached it may be formally drawn up as a Deed of Separation by solicitors and signed by the couple.

The Family Mediation Service is state funded and is free but only operates in Dublin. There are also mediators in private practice.

SEXUAL OFFENCES

Buggery (Sodomy)

Sodomy is defined as the penetration, by the penis, of the anus of a man or woman. In 1981, the law governing homosexual practices (indecent assault, gross indecency, buggery, etc.) was challenged in the Supreme Court case *Norris* v. *A-G*, on the grounds that it offended the constitution e.g. interfered with a right to privacy and the right to freedom of expression, was discriminatory in that female homosexuals were treated differently, etc. The challenge was unsuccessful. The Christian nature of the state (and the constitution) entitled the legislature to criminalise behaviour regarded as being morally wrong by the Christian churches. The legislature was also entitled to treat male homosexuality and female homosexuality differently.

With the passing of the Criminal Law (Sexual Offences) Act, 1993 significant changes were introduced in this area. This Act abolished the offence of buggery between persons over the age of seventeen years. It retains buggery as an offence where it involves a person under the age of seventeen years. The maximum sentence for buggery in such circumstances is life imprisonment, with a five-year term of imprisonment for attempted buggery in the case of a first conviction and ten years in the case of a second or any subsequent conviction. Where a person commits or attempts to commit an act of buggery with a person who is mentally impaired the maximum sentence is imprisonment for a period of ten years.

The offence of gross indecency between men over the age of seventeen years created by the Criminal Law Act, 1885 was abolished by the Criminal Law (Sexual Offences) Act, 1993.

Bestiality

Bestiality is defined as vaginal or anal intercourse by a man or a woman with an animal. The maximum penalty under the 1861 Act is penal servitude for life and, in the case of an attempt, ten years' penal servitude.

Gross Indecency

This covers homosexual acts between consenting males which fall short of buggery but go beyond mere indecency.

Acts of gross indecency between females were not referred to in the 1885 Act, indicating that the practice of homosexual acts between males was an offence whereas between females it was not. The belief, at the time of passing of this Act, attributed supposedly to Queen Victoria was that there was no such thing as a female homosexual.

Incest

By Males

A male person who has sexual intercourse with a female who is, to his knowledge, his mother, daughter, granddaughter or sister, is guilty of incest. This offence is punishable by up to twenty years' imprisonment under the 1993 Criminal Justice Act.

If it is proved that the girl is under fifteen years of age, the penalty is penal servitude for life or two years' imprisonment.

Attempting to commit this offence carries a penalty of up to two years' imprisonment.

It is immaterial that sexual intercourse took place with the consent of the female. In the absence of consent, however, the more serious charge of rape applies.

By Females

A female of seventeen years or over who permits her grandfather, father, son or brother to have sexual intercourse with her is guilty of incest. It is punishable by penal servitude for a term not more than seven years and not less than three, or two years' imprisonment. Incest cases are tried 'in camera', that is, in the absence of the public.

Prostitution

Soliciting for the purposes of prostitution is an offence for which the penalty is a fine of £250 for the first conviction, £500 in the case of a second conviction, and £500 or imprisonment for a term not exceeding four weeks, or both, in the case of a third or subsequent conviction.

Loitering for the purposes of prostitution, i.e. kerb crawling, is an offence under the Criminal Law (Sexual Offences) Act, 1993 if after being asked to move on by a garda the driver refuses to do so. Penalties are a fine of £250 for a first conviction, £500 in the case of a second conviction and £500 or imprisonment for a term not exceeding four weeks, or both, in the case of a third or subsequent conviction.

Pimps

Controlling or directing the activities of a prostitute or prostitutes or coercing a person to be a prostitute is an offence for which the maximum penalty is a fine of £10,000 or imprisonment for a term of five years, or both.

Living on the Earnings of Prostitution

A person who lives on the earnings of the prostitution of another *and* aids and abets that prostitution is liable to a fine of up to £1,000 and/or imprisonment for a term of up to six months, or both.

Brothels

Keeping a brothel or allowing one's premises to be used as a brothel is an offence for which the maximum penalty is a fine of £10,000 or imprisonment for up to five years, or both.

Rape and Sexual Assault

Rape

A man commits rape if he has sexual intercourse with a woman who, at the time, does not consent and at that time he knows that she does not consent or he is reckless as to whether she does or does not consent.

A new crime 'Rape under Section 4' was introduced in the 1990 Criminal Law (Rape) Act. These so called 'Section 4' rapes cover sexual assaults that include:

(1) Penetration (however slight) of anus or mouth by the penis.

(2) Penetration (however slight) of the vagina by any object.

The victim in (1) may be a male or female and the perpetrator in (2) may be male or female.

The penalty for rape and rape under Section 4 is penal servitude for life. Cases are tried in the Central Criminal Court in the absence of the public.

Marital Rape
Rape within marriage is now a recognised crime under Irish law. The rule that a husband could not be guilty of the rape of his wife was abolished by the 1990 Act. In these cases, proceedings will not be instituted except by or with the consent of the DPP.

Age of Accused
The rule of law that a boy under the age of fourteen was incapable of committing a sexual offence was abolished by the 1990 Act.

Aggravated Sexual Assault
Aggravated sexual assault is a sexual assault that involves serious violence or the threat of serious violence or causes injury, humiliation or degradation of a grave nature to the victim, male or female. The penalty is life imprisonment. Cases are tried in the Central Criminal Court in the absence of the public.

Sexual Assault
A sexual assault is an indecent assault upon a male or female which is less serious than the offence of aggravated sexual assault. The penalty is imprisonment for up to five years. Boys under fourteen years and women are legally capable of committing these offences.

Unlawful Carnal Knowledge
By Reason of Age
Having sexual intercourse with a girl under fifteen years of age is an offence for which the maximum penalty is penal servitude for life or imprisonment for up to two years.

Where the girl is over fifteen but under seventeen years of age the offence is punishable by penal servitude for up to five years or imprisonment for up to two years.

Consent, on the part of the girl, or the belief that the girl is over fifteen or seventeen years cannot be relied on as defences to a charge.

By Reason of Mental Handicap
Having sexual intercourse, in circumstances which do not amount to rape, with a woman who is mentally handicapped where the accused knew of the woman's state of mind, is an offence for which the penalty is ten years' imprisonment. Where the woman was in the care of the accused, the penalty is higher.

Giving Evidence in Certain Proceedings
Introduced in the Criminal Evidence Act, 1992 is the provision whereby in cases involving a sexual offence or an offence involving violence or the threat of violence, a person (other than the accused) who is under seventeen years of age may give evidence to a court through a live television link.

SMALL CLAIMS PROCEDURE

The District Courts (SCP) Rules, 1991 came into operation on 10 December 1991. These rules provide an alternative method of commencing and dealing with a civil proceeding in respect of a small claim, to be known as the Small Claims Procedure. The rules allow for the Small Claims Procedure to operate in Dublin, Cork and in Sligo. A small claim means any civil proceeding commenced by a consumer against a vendor in relation to any goods or service purchased in which the amount of the claim does not exceed the sum of £500 and which is not a claim

(a) arising under the Hire Purchase Acts, 1946 and 1960, *or*

(b) arising from a breach of a leasing arrangement.

An application under these rules should be in writing and shall be lodged with the Small Claims Registrar at the District Court office in Dublin, Cork or Sligo together with a fee of £5. The person making the claim may call to the court office for assistance in completing the application form. The Registrar shall record particulars of each such claim in the book to be known as the Small Claims Register. It is open to the Registrar to interview the claimant to record the full facts of the claim. If the Registrar considers the claim to be inappropriate to the Small Claims Procedure he will contact the claimant and inform him of the position and will refund £5. If the respondent, that is, the person against whom the claim is made, admits the claim against him and

(a) agrees to pay the amount claimed, *or*

(b) consents to judgment being given against him or wishes to pay the amount claimed by instalments,

he completes the Notice of Acceptance of Liability form within fifteen days of the service of the notice of claim and copy claim on him. If the amount is paid the Registrar records the supplement in the Small Claims Register.

If the respondent consents to judgment, the Registrar avails of the summary judgment rules to recover the amount outstanding.

Finally, where the respondent wishes to pay the amount claimed by instalments, the Registrar seeks the consent of the applicant to the terms intended by the respondent. The Small Claims Registrar will make every effort to settle the dispute between the parties and with that end in mind he may interview them and any other person whom either party might wish him to hear. Under the rules it is not open to the Registrar to award costs or witnesses' expenses to anyone when determining a claim. The claimant and respondent are liable for their own legal costs and expenses.

STRIKES

The law in relation to strikes is governed primarily by statute with various case law amplifying the interpretations of certain statutes. Statutes involved principally are the Trade Union Acts, 1941-75 and the Industrial Relations Act, 1990. The Industrial Relations Act, 1990 was passed into law in July 1990 and it repealed the Trade Disputes Act of 1906 in its entirety. Like the 1906 Trade Disputes Act it provides immunity to trade unions and their members for certain acts done in contemplation or in furtherance of a trade dispute. It makes peaceful picketing legal in certain circumstances. It also contains a very important provision that every trade union must contain in its rules a rule requiring a secret ballot before a strike or industrial action can be authorised.

How does the Industrial Relations Act Operate?

This Act renders lawful a number of activities which may be undertaken by a trade union and its workers in the furtherance or in the contemplation of a trade dispute. For this immunity to apply the following conditions must be met:
(i)   there must be a trade dispute;
(ii) the action must be permitted by the Act;
(iii) the action must not have been rejected by a ballot of the workers concerned;
(iv) if the action concerns one individual worker, then agreed procedures normally used in that employment must have been used and exhausted.

What is the Definition of a Trade Dispute?

It is defined in the Act as 'any dispute between employers and workers which is connected with the employment or non-employment, or the terms or conditions of or affecting the employment of any person'. While this definition is fairly self-explanatory, it must be noted that the dispute must be between employers and workers. Any dispute which is purely between workers is not regarded as a trade dispute. The Act defines an employer as 'any person for whom one or more workers work or have worked or normally work or seek to work having previously worked for that person' and the Act defines a worker as any person who is/was employed whether or not in the employment of the employer with whom a trade dispute arises, but *does not include a member of the Defence Forces or of the Garda Síochána.*

What Matters Constitute a Trade Dispute?

The Act states that the dispute must be concerned with 'the employment or non-employment, or the terms or conditions of, or affecting the employment of any person'. It would certainly appear that the following issues are covered by the Act: dismissal, non-employment, range of duties, recognition of trade unions, pay and conditions, physical conditions of work and improvement of statutory conditions.

Are there any Matters which cannot be the subject of a Trade Dispute?

Yes. For example, there cannot be a valid trade dispute aimed at forcing workers to join a union against their wishes. Similarly, a dispute which is connected with a political issue only could not be a valid trade dispute. One cannot have a trade dispute telling an employer how to run his business. It should also be noted that the Act only applies to trade unions which hold a negotiating licence under the Trade Unions Acts, 1941-90.

What Activities can be carried on where there is a Trade Dispute?

The Act allows workers during a lawful trade dispute to:
   (i) encourage other workers to break their contract of employment;
   (ii) threaten to break a contract of employment or threaten to encourage others to do so;
   (iii) interfere with the trade or business of others or the right of others to dispose of their capital or labour as they see fit.

Should Notice be Served on the Employer?

Yes. During a strike a person's contract of employment is suspended. This only operates if notice of the same length as would be required to terminate the contract is given to the employer. Under the Minimum Notice and Terms of Employment Act, 1973 the Notice is one week. However, there may be various agreements which would then necessitate a longer period. If the adequate notice is not given the strike is not lawful.

Are there any Activities which may not be Undertaken?

Yes. A union may not call upon the workers to neglect any work which they are obliged by statute to perform. They may not also cause a direct inducement of a breach of a commercial contract. It is also unlawful for a union to call upon its workers to withhold money or property which is in trust to them for the benefit of their employer. This brings us to the question of picketing. The Act makes provision for primary picketing and secondary picketing.

Primary Picketing is defined thus in the Act: 'It shall be lawful for one or more persons, acting on their own behalf or on behalf of a trade union in contemplation or furtherance of a trade dispute, to attend at, or where that is not practicable, at the approaches to, a place where their employer works or carries on business if they so attend merely for the purpose of peacefully obtaining or communicating information or peacefully persuading any person to work or abstain from working.' The following points arise:

- *(i)* the picket can only take place in contemplation or furtherance of a trade dispute;
- *(ii)* only employees of the employer in the dispute may picket;
- *(iii)* the picket must be at a place where the employer in dispute works or carries on business;
- *(iv)* picketing must be peaceful.

There is one exception to the rule that only employees of the employer in the dispute must picket: a trade union official may accompany his or her members on the picket line. The picket can be mounted at any premises where the employer in dispute works or carries on business. It need not actually be the premises at which the workers in dispute are employed. Neither does it have to be a premises owned by the employer provided the employer was undertaking work or carrying on business from that premises. If one is picketing in an industrial estate or a shopping centre it is essential that the placards identify the particular employer in dispute.

The Act defines *secondary picketing* thus: 'It shall be lawful for one or more persons acting on their own behalf or on behalf of a trade union in contemplation or furtherance of a trade dispute, to attend at, or where that is not practicable, at the approaches to, a place where the employer who is not a party to the trade dispute works or carries on business if, but only if, it is reasonable for those who are so attending to believe at the commencement of their attendance and throughout the continuance of their attendance that that employer has directly assisted their employer who is a party to the trade dispute for the purpose of frustrating the strike or other industrial action, provided that such attendance is merely for the purpose of peacefully obtaining or communicating information, or of peacefully persuading any person to work or abstain from working.' As you will see it is fundamental for immunity to be obtained under this section that the picketers had reasonable grounds for believing that that employer being picketed had provided direct assistance to their employer for the purpose of frustrating a strike or other industrial action in which they are engaged. It has to be emphasised in this regard that the help given by the other employer must be for the purpose of *frustrating the strike.* One can certainly envisage that this is an area where a substantial volume of case law will develop.

Balloting

Since 18 July 1992 it is essential that every trade union must contain a provision in its rules that that union cannot organise, participate or sanction or support a strike without a secret ballot of its members who it is reasonable to believe will be called upon to engage in the strike. Every member of the union who is likely to be engaged in the strike must be given an opportunity of voting. The conduct of the ballot must be without interference. The union itself may decide how to conduct the ballot, whether by postal vote, by a ballot at the workplace or by convening a general meeting for the purpose. It is essential that reasonable notice of the ballot be given if it is intended to call a general meeting. After the ballot the union must make known the following:

  (*a*) the number of ballots issued;
  (*b*) the number of votes cast;
  (*c*) the number of votes in favour of the proposal;
  (*d*) the number of votes against, and
  (*e*) the number of spoilt votes.

If a secret ballot has taken place and there is a majority decision against strike action the protection of the Act will not apply if the union proceeds with the strike. Nor will it apply if a minority of those who participated in the ballot go on strike unofficially. In these cases an injunction may be granted by the court and the union could also be liable for damages.

TRESPASS

There are three types of trespass:
- **(1)** Trespass to the person;
- **(2)** Trespass to goods;
- **(3)** Trespass to land.

Trespass is actionable per se. This means that the defendant, or person causing the trespass, is liable once the right of the plaintiff has been interfered with, even though there is no actual damage. Therefore, it can be said that liability for trespass is strict. In other civil wrongs, it is often necessary to prove injury to the person or damage to the property before it is open to a person to recover, but not in trespass.

Let us look at each one in turn.

Trespass to the Person:

This may result in (*a*) assault, (*b*) battery or (*c*) false imprisonment.

Assault

This is an attempt or threat to apply unlawful force to the person of another, whereby that other person is put in fear of violence. Examples of this are striking at another with a stick or a fist or throwing a stone or bottle. Mere words are not sufficient to constitute an assault. However, words may prevent what in other circumstances would amount to an assault, for example, in a very old case called *Tubervill* v. *Savage* (1669), a man laid his hand on his sword and said 'if it were not court time I would not take such language from you'. This was held not to be an assault.

Battery

Battery consists of applying force, however slight, to the person of another. The charge of battery is usually combined with assault, namely assault and battery. Examples of battery are as follows: throwing water or fruit at a person, spitting in his face, holding him by the arm or shoulder, or giving a person a black eye.

False Imprisonment

False imprisonment consists of wrongful deprivation of personal liberty in any form. As with assault and battery, false imprisonment is actionable per se, that is, without proof of injury or damage. Force need not be used to constitute false imprisonment. The threat of force may, however, be sufficient; for example, 'stay there or I will shoot you', may be sufficient to ground an action for false imprisonment.

The deprivation of liberty or the restraint must be total and complete. Thus to restrain a person from going in three ways but leaving him free to go in a fourth way is not false imprisonment. This is shown in a case called *Bird* v. *Jones* (1845). A footpath on Hammersmith Bridge in London was lawfully blocked to allow for the erection of a grandstand for a boat race. The grandstand effectively prevented the plaintiff from making his way along that section of the bridge. He refused to move to the other side of the bridge to continue his journey and he sued for false imprisonment. Held by the court that there was no false imprisonment since the plaintiff was free to go another way.

The laying of a hand on the arm or shoulder of a person, or the restraining of a person is not necessarily actionable and, in fact, may provide a defence to an action for trespass to the person. For example, the following would be viewed as good defences to such an action:

  (i) self-defence;
  (ii) defence of property;
  (iii) parental authority;
  (iv) judicial authority; and finally,
  (v) preservation of the peace.

It is lawful for a person to defend himself against an assault or battery. However, the defence used must bear some proportion to the attack. The person defending himself should use no more force than is necessary or reasonable in the circumstances. For example, if John throws an apple at Tom, it is not open to Tom to allege that he defended himself by striking Tom repeatedly with a stick or some such weapon. Similar rules apply to the defence of one's property, including a house. It is open to an occupier to use reasonable force to eject a trespasser.

A parent may chastise his child but, again, the chastisement must be reasonable. If it goes beyond what is reasonable, it may amount to the criminal offence of cruelty to a child. Corporal punishment is not permitted in schools.

A judge may issue a bench warrant to a member of the garda síochána and it is open to the garda to use reasonable force to apprehend the person named in the warrant. Again, the force used must be reasonable. Likewise, all persons owe a duty not to disturb the public peace. The gardaí have wide common law and statutory powers to make arrests, to enforce the law and to preserve the peace. Even though the gardaí are involved, they are under an obligation not to use more force than is necessary in the circumstances.

Trespass to Land

Trespass to land may take three forms:
  (a) entering on the land of another;
  (b) remaining on the land of another;
  (c) throwing or placing any object upon the land of another.

This tort, or civil wrong, is actionable per se and it is not necessary to prove actual damage to the land. Land may be defined as not only the soil itself but things under the soil and buildings or houses affixed to the surface of the soil. There is a general rule that the owner of the land owns all the land below the surface and all the space above the land; exceptions involve Air Navigation Acts, etc. Therefore, trespass may occur by burrowing into the soil, for example, to lay a cable or to take gravel from another's land.

Examples of trespass to land include putting a hand on a fence or through an open window of a house or throwing stones onto another's land. To allow slates from a derelict house to fall onto a neighbour's land is not trespass but may constitute a nuisance. The sign 'trespassers will be prosecuted' is not accurate. Mere trespass on land is not a crime and no prosecution for it may be brought, though a civil action may be. In civil trespass, no damage need be proved. A person may be sued even though he did not know he was trespassing for mistake is no defence. It is embodied in the maxim 'Ignorance of the law is no defence.' Trespass is fundamentally a wrong against possession, not against ownership. Therefore, an owner out of possession cannot sue. For example, a landlord who enters lands leased may be in breach of the agreement between himself and the tenant and may be liable in trespass to the tenant.

Justification for Entering

We have noted that to constitute actionable trespass, an entry on land must be unlawful. There are, however, instances where the 'trespasser' may claim that his entry is justifiable either by common law or by statute. Entry by lawful authority—for example, by the gardaí to make an arrest or to search premises—is a case in point, as is entry to abate a nuisance. This means self-help: the injured party stops the nuisance by removing the cause; abatement is not favoured as a remedy by the law. Entry may be made to retake goods owned by the 'trespasser' provided the goods are placed there by the occupier of the land or possibly by a third party. Then there is entry by licence or permission of the occupier. A licence is 'that consent which, without passing any interest in the property to which it relates, merely prevents the acts for which consent is given from being wrongful' and, finally, peaceable entry on the land by a person entitled to possession of it. The following remedies are available to a person who believes that his property has been trespassed upon:

(1) Injunction: this may be used to prevent the continuance or repetition of the acts of trespass. Damages may be sought as a result of the trespass. Damages are assessed on the amount the land is diminished as a result of the trespass.

(2) Ejection: the occupier of the land may eject the trespasser after first requesting him to leave and then allowing him peaceably to do so. Reasonable force is the force that may be used to eject the trespasser, otherwise the occupier may find himself sued for assault and battery.

Trespass *ab initio*

Where a person enters the lands of another by authority, he may become a trespasser if, by his subsequent actions, he abuses his right of entry. This is known as trespass *ab initio* and is illustrated by the very old case known as The Six Carpenters.

In 1610 six carpenters entered the Queen's Head Inn, Cripplegate, and consumed a quart of wine (7d) and some bread (1d) for which they refused to pay. The question for the court was whether their non-payment made the entry tortious, so as to enable them to be sued in trespass. The court held that 'When entry, authority or licence is given to any one by the law, and he doth abuse it, he shall be a trespasser *ab initio*.' The rule is that the authority, having been abused by doing a wrongful act under cover of it, is cancelled retrospectively so that the exercise of it becomes actionable as a trespass.

Trespass to Goods

Trespass to goods is the intention or negligent interference with the possession of goods of another. Trespass to goods is action-able per se. Examples of trespass to goods include throwing another's goods out of a window; removing a motorbike from a shed; shifting a dustbin.

To maintain an action of trespass to goods, the person taking the action must show that he had possession of the goods at the time of the trespass. Therefore, a borrower or a hirer of goods may maintain such an action against any person who wrongfully interferes with the goods in his possession. An example is a shoe-maker to whom shoes are sent for repair.

Trespass to goods may be by way of *detinue* or *conversion*. Detinue means the wrongful detention of the goods of another. For example, if John lends his book to Tom for one week only and Tom refuses to return it when the week elapses, that is detinue. Or, if Mary leaves her shoes into Jack to be repaired and he later declines to return them after a demand has been made for their return, an action in detinue is available. Therefore, in detinue, the person claiming the goods must be the owner of the goods and not merely a possessor. There must have been a demand for the return of the goods and a refusal to return them. Detinue is the proper remedy where the person requires restitution of the specif-ic or actual goods either loaned or left in for repair.

Conversion consists in the wilful and wrongful interference with the goods of another. Conversion may be committed by tak-ing, by detention, by wrongful delivery and by destruction. Where someone takes the goods out of the possession of another without lawful justification, that person may be sued in conversion. Every simple theft or stealing, for example, where Tom steals Mary's watch, is a conversion. However, the shifting of goods from one place to another may be trespass but is not conversion. Where a person detains the goods of another without justification, the per-son may sue in conversion if he wants damages. If he wants the actual goods returned, he may sue in detinue, as above. If a per-son, without lawful justification, delivers goods belonging to another to a total stranger, that person may be responsible in conversion.

Finally, if a person wilfully and unlawfully destroys the goods of another, this may amount to conversion. There must be a complete destruction of the goods: damage is insufficient. In 1722, a chimney sweep's boy found a jewel and handed it to a jeweller who took the jewel from its setting and refused to return it to the boy who, there-upon, sued the jeweller in conversion. Held by the court that the jeweller was liable because the finder, that is the boy, had a good title except as against the true owner. Finally, the chief difference between detinue and conversion is that in detinue the civil wrong (or tort) comprises a *denial of possession* to the owner; in conversion, there must be some act involving *denial of title.*

TRUSTS

The original intention or function of a trust was tax avoidance. Even in modern times a trust retains this original function. The trust is an important device for the solicitor in trying to redistribute the property of his wealthy clients so as to reduce the effects of modern tax systems. The trust reduces the tax liability and, at the same time, keeps the property within the family ownership.

A trust has been defined as 'an equitable obligation imposing upon a person (who is called a trustee) the duty of dealing with property over which he has control (which is called the trust property) for the benefit of persons (who are called beneficiaries) of whom he may himself be one and any one of whom may enforce'.

Generally speaking, all kinds of property may be held in trust but, in practice, most trust property includes land, shares and stocks. Today, trusts are employed widely for protecting the interest of those who from legal or physical incapacity, are unable to look after themselves or their affairs. Examples of trusts are as follows:

- *(a)* trusts for the benefit of minors—persons under eighteen years;
- *(b)* trusts for the benefit of persons suffering from physical or mental incapacity;
- *(c)* trusts for the benefit of clubs;
- *(d)* trusts for charitable purposes.

The distinctive feature of the trust is the duality of ownership. The property is owned by two persons, namely the trustee and the beneficiary. The trustee is looked upon as the legal owner and the beneficiary is the equitable owner. A trust can come into effect either by the owner of the property disposing of it by will, or by an instrument intended to take effect in his lifetime. The second one is called a disposition inter vivos. In the first case, the creator of the trust is called a testator as it arose by virtue of his will; in the second situation, the creator is called a settler. Originally, land was the usual subject matter of trusts but any form of property—money, shares in a company, copyrights and patents—may be. A trust may be expressly created or it may arise by operation of law.

A private express trust is one expressly created by the settler inter vivos, that is, during life or by will for the benefit of one person or a group of persons. It may be established be deed, in writing, by will or merely orally in certain cases. It was laid down in *Knight* v. *Knight* (1840), that three certainties are necessary for the creation of a trust:

  (i) certainty of intention;
  (ii) certainty of subject matter;
  (iii) certainty of objects.

Certainty of Intention
Here the creator must show by his words that a trust is created. The words must be imperative: there must be a positive command that a thing shall be done and that a trust shall be created.

Certainty of Subject Matter
This refers to the property, land, money, copyright or patents to which the trust is to apply. There must be no ambiguity or uncertainty. If there is, the intended trust will fail.

Certainty of Objects
This means the persons whom the trust is intended to benefit. Such persons must be identified with certainty and the interests which they are to take must be discoverable.

Public Trusts
There are other trusts called public or charitable trusts and these may be

  (i) for the relief of poverty;
  (ii) for the advancement of education;
  (iii) for the advancement of religion;
  (iv) for other purposes beneficial to the community.

However, no trust can be described as charitable unless it is of a public nature. That is, it must benefit the public as a whole or at least a section of it. Attempts have been made to establish public or charitable trusts for the old and the disabled, for purposes of health, for recreation facilities, for animals and for political objects. Under political objects, the Fianna Fail Party in Ireland and, in England, the Conservative and Labour Parties have failed to qualify as charitable objects.

An example of a trust which was created for purposes beneficial to the community and not falling under any of the three preceding headings, namely relief or poverty, the advancement of education and the advancement of religion, is the Bolton Trust, established by the staff of Dublin Institute of Technology which consists of a number of colleges in Dublin, for example College of Technology, Bolton Street; College of Technology, Kevin Street; College of Commerce, Rathmines; College of Catering, Cathal Brugha Street; College of Marketing and Design, Mountjoy Square; and the College of Music. The trust provides services for start-up enterprises. The trust draws on the expertise of the lecturers in the above named Colleges and this has proved to be of immeasurable benefit to those commencing businesses who have had no previous experience. Up to December 1991, twenty-four companies and ninety-eight jobs were created. The Bolton Trust was greatly encouraged by these results and looks forward to building on the success into the future.

Cy Pres

A word concerning the cy pres doctrine. Occasionally it is impossible to carry out the intentions of the person who makes a gift to charity as the charity has ceased to exist and, in that situation, the court will set up the trust cy pres; from 'si pres', meaning 'so near'. In other words, it will apply the gift to some other charity as near as possible to the original purpose named by the donor.

The cy pres doctrine was applied with reference to the Royal Hospital, Kilmainham. The hospital was established by King Charles II in 1684 for the support and maintenance of old soldiers. It was endowed with substantial lands overlooking the River Liffey. It ceased to function as a hospital after 1921, the remaining tenants being transferred to the Royal Hospital Chelsea, England and the building and lands vested in the Irish government. There were, however, funds in court representing compensation paid to the hospital for some of the land which had been required for Kingsbridge railway station now Heuston station. A question arose as to how the monies should be applied and, finally, the Royal Hospital Kilmainham Act, 1961 was passed which provided that the High Court must order certain sums to be made out of the income of the funds to the Royal Hospital Chelsea, and also to settle a scheme for some charitable purposes for the benefit of the Irish Defence Forces.

The day-to-day running of charities is under the supervision of the Commissioners for Charitable Donations and Requests. The commissioners have power to commence proceedings to recover charitable funds that have been misapplied. However, they must have the consent of the Attorney-General. The commissioners have a general power to authorise or direct the taking of proceedings in any charitable matter or to indicate to the Attorney-General that such proceedings should be commenced.

Duties of Trustees

We now deal with the duties of trustees. The main duties falling upon a trustee are to administer the trust property prudently and comply strictly with the terms of the trust. The trustee must take the same care of the trust property as a prudent man would take of his own property. If he is careless in administering the trust, he may be personally held liable for losses. He must collect all debts owing to the trust and he may take legal action to recover debts owed to the trust. The trustee must not profit from his position and if he does make a profit, he may be compelled to refund any such profit to the beneficiaries. Generally speaking, he may not delegate his duties although there are some occasions when he may do so. He is obliged to keep proper accounts and must produce them for inspection by a beneficiary. Finally, a trustee is not permitted to charge for his services unless so authorised. The authorisation may be contained within the instrument setting up the trust or may be given by all of the beneficiaries, if of full age and capacity, or by a court.

There are a number of ways in which a trusteeship may be terminated by disclaimer. There is no compulsion on a trustee to accept office. He may decline to accept the position of trustee. If he wishes to disclaim, he must do so quickly, otherwise a presumption may arise that he has accepted the position. It is not open to a trustee to disclaim part of the trust: he must disclaim all or nothing.

Removal

A trustee may be removed from office under express power contained in a will of deed or under statute or by the court, where the trustee commits a fraud on the beneficiaries, or where the trustee becomes bankrupt.

Retirement

Once a trustee has accepted his appointment he cannot retire save in limited circumstances. He may retire if he gets the consent of his co-trustees or any person who is empowered to appoint trustees. A trustee may also obtain his discharge by application to the court and, finally, he may retire if he obtains the consent of all the beneficiaries who are competent to give such a consent.

Replacement

A trustee may be replaced by a new trustee. The power of replacement is exercisable by the person named in the trust or, if no such persons are named, by the remaining trustees.

UNFAIR DISMISSALS ACTS, 1977, 1991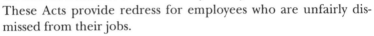

These Acts provide redress for employees who are unfairly dismissed from their jobs.

Who is Covered?

Employees who have at least one year's continuous service with the employer involved and who are normally expected to work at least eight hours a week are covered. Where the dismissal is for pregnancy or trade union activity the one year's service is not a requirement. The eight-hour limit means that part-time employees are protected.

Certain categories of employees are excluded from the protection of the Act. These include:

- Gardaí, Defence Forces
- civil servants (except specified industrial grades)
- officers of a health board, local authority, VEC or a committee of agriculture.
- FAS trainees or apprentices
- persons undergoing training for the purpose of becoming qualified as a nurse, pharmacist, medical laboratory technician, physiotherapist, social worker, etc.
- persons who have reached retiring age
- close relatives of the employer who live and work in his/her residence or farm.

What is Dismissal?

The act covers three situations:

(1) Where the employer terminates the employment with or without notice. If notice is given it should be worked through. Otherwise you will be treated as having terminated the employment yourself and, therefore, a claim for unfair dismissals may not be taken. However, in some circumstances employers' behaviour may entitle an employee to walk out. If so, constructive dismissal applies.

(2) Constructive dismissal. This arises where the employer's behaviour is so unreasonable that you feel obliged to resign, the conduct constitutes a significant breach of the contract, or the employer shows that s/he no longer intends to be bound by the terms of that contract. In this case it is the employee who terminates the employment.

The main problem with this situation is that the dividing line between a constructive dismissal and a voluntary resignation can be a very fine one.

(3) Where the contract of employment is for a fixed term or a fixed purpose and the employer refuses to renew.

Reasons for Dismissal

Reasons which are automatically unfair

 (*i*)   Trade union membership and activity.
 (*ii*) Religious or political beliefs.
 (*iii*) Participating in criminal or civil proceedings taken against the employer.
 (*iv*) Race or colour.
 (*v*)   Pregnancy or matters connected with it.

All dismissals are presumed to be unfair and it is up to an employer to prove otherwise. To do this s/he must show that the dismissal was for a 'fair reason' and in the particular set of circumstances that dismissal was justified.

Fair Reasons for Dismissal

 (*i*)   Lack of capability, competence, qualifications, inadequate health for the job you are employed to do.
 (*ii*) Conduct. This might be one serious incident or a series of less serious but unacceptable acts. Fighting, abuse of sick leave, repeated refusal to obey reasonable instructions: all have been held to constitute conduct warranting dismissal. It should be noted that in some circumstances, conduct outside work may be taken into account. Acting in deliberate conflict of interest with an employer is an example.
 (*iii*) Where continuation of employment will contravene another law, e.g. employing a worker who is found to be under age.
 (*iv*) Redundancy, provided that appropriate selection procedures are followed.

Remedies

An employee who has been found to be unfairly dismissed will be awarded either re-instatement, re-engagement or compensation. It is the Rights Commissioners, a tribunal or a court which on an appeal will decide on the appropriate form of redress.

Re-instatement Essentially this means that the employee must be treated as though the dismissal had not taken place. Such an award is generally made only in cases where it is accepted that the employee did not contribute to the dismissal in any way.

Re-engagement This means that the employee is given a similar 'suitable' job subject to conditions that are reasonable in the circumstances. This usually arises in cases where it is considered that the employee is partly culpable. Pay resumes when the employee resumes work.

Compensation Most successful claims for unfair dismissal result in awards of compensation. The amount may not exceed 104 weeks' remuneration. Regard must be had to financial loss which includes actual and prospective loss, loss of pension and other employment rights. Awards may be reduced where an employee contributed to his/her own dismissal or failed to mitigate the loss resulting from dismissal by, for example, not seeking alternative employment.

Taking a Claim

The employee notifies a Rights Commissioner (Form 2) or the Employment Appeals Tribunal (Form RP51A) within six months of the date of dismissal. A copy of the notice must be given to the employer within the same six-month period.

If the initial claim was to a Rights Commissioner and that Commissioner's recommendation is not accepted, the employer fails to comply with it or the employer objects to the hearing by the Commissioner, an appeal may be taken to the tribunal. There is a strict time limit of six weeks for this. A notice must be given to the employer within the same six-week period.

In the case of either a claim or an appeal to the tribunal the employer must lodge a statement of defence within fourteen days of receipt of notice from the tribunal that it is to hear the case.

The case goes to the Circuit Court if:
– either party appeals the tribunal's decision *or*
– the Minister for Labour decides to proceed against an employer for non-compliance with the decision of the tribunal.

Costs

Both parties must pay their own costs whether successful or otherwise. However, on an appeal to the Circuit Court, a judge may award costs in favour of the successful person.

A new Bill in this area is under consideration and when enacted will effect considerable changes to the current law.

VIDEOS

Supplying, or offering to supply, videos without complying with the regulations governing videos is an offence for which the penalty is on summary conviction a £1,000 fine and/or twelve months', or on conviction on indictment a fine and/or three years' imprisonment.

The official Censor will not declare works fit for viewing which would in his opinion:

(i) cause persons to commit crime;

(ii) stir up hatred against a group on account of their race, colour, nationality, religion, ethnic or national origins, membership of the travelling community or sexual orientation; *or*

(iii) would lend, by reason of the inclusion in it of obscene matter, to deprave or corrupt persons who might view it; *or*

(iv) if they depict acts of gross violence or cruelty towards humans or animals.

Permitting the viewing of videos which do not comply with law is an offence for which the penalty is a £1,000 fine.

There is a Register of Prohibited Video Works maintained by the Official Censor which may be inspected by the public free of charge. There is also a Register of Video Wholesale Licences and a Register of Video Retail Licences which may be inspected.

VOTING

Electorate

Every Irish and British citizen over eighteen years of age whose name has been entered in the register of electors is entitled to vote in Dáil elections, European Parliament elections and local government elections. A national of a member state of the European Community (other than Britain) is entitled to be registered as a European Parliament and local government elector only. Any other person over eighteen years, ordinarily resident in the state, is entitled to be registered as a local government elector only. The register is updated annually with the new register coming into force on 15 April each year.

The electorate in Seanad elections is restricted to particular groups of people. There are sixty members in the Seanad, eleven of whom are nominated by the Taoiseach and forty-nine of whom are elected. Of that forty-nine, six represent the National University of Ireland (three members) and Dublin University (three members) and are elected by the graduates of those universities. The electorate for the National University of Ireland numbers about 80,000, while the Trinity electorate is around 20,000. The electorate for the remaining forty-three seats is made up of members of the Dáil, the outgoing Seanad and the various county councils and other local authorities.

WARRANTIES

In addition to guarantees, it is often necessary to distinguish between a condition and a warranty in a contract. A condition is a fundamental term within the contract. For example, if the television set you have purchased does not work, you can repudiate, set aside or call off the bargain or contract and claim compensation for the actual monetary loss and perhaps something more for the inconvenience caused and for your costs. A warranty is often a term collateral to the main purpose of the contract which does not entitle a party who is dissatisfied with the contract to repudiate it or to set it aside. For example, if a second-hand motor car which was claimed to be in perfect working order, required a new gear box compensation would be awarded for the actual loss. But the contract would not be entirely set aside and the full amount of money would not be returnable. Whether a term is a condition or a warranty depends on the construction of the contract as a whole.

The distinction between a condition and a warranty can be important in that if the seller of goods breaches a condition the purchaser has a choice of action. The buyer can treat the contract as satisfied or repudiated, return the goods or refuse to accept them and ask for the return of his money or refuse to pay for the goods. It is also open to the purchaser to treat the breach of the condition as though it were a breach of warranty. If there is a breach of warranty by the seller, the purchaser is not usually entitled to reject the goods. Instead, the purchaser may claim that the breach of warranty reduces the price or he may sue the seller for damages for loss which results from the breach of the warranty.

WARRANTS

A warrant is an authority or permission to:
- (*i*)   arrest a person;
- (*ii*) search a premises;
- (*iii*) levy for the non-payment of a legal penalty.

Arrest

The warrant should state the offence concerned, the person to be arrested, the place of issue, the date, etc. Where the name of the person to be arrested is unknown, a description in as much detail as possible should be given. The garda should have the warrant in his/her possession when making the arrest. An exception to this is where the arrest is made because a person has failed to appear in court in accordance with his/her bail. This type of warrant is known as a bench warrant. A warrant will only be issued where the offence is a serious one (indictable). For summary offences a summons is used (*see* page 17). A garda may use reasonable force to execute an arrest warrant. A warrant for a person charged with an indictable offence, or who has failed to appear in court, remains valid until it is executed.

Seizure of Evidence on Arrest

Gardaí may seize property in the custody or possession of the person arrested if they believe it necessary to do so to avoid its destruction; and that it is evidence supporting the charge upon which the arrest is made, or some other criminal charge; or where it is reasonably believed that the property is stolen.

Warrant to Search a Premises

Numerous Acts grant the power to issue warrants for this purpose. The conditions and terms vary from Act to Act. Where warrants are issued there are time limits for enforcing them. Warrants can be granted by a District Court or a Peace Commissioner.

Warrants issued for Non-Payment of a Legal Duty

These are usually issued for the purpose of payment of a penalty or a debt. They may involve the seizure of goods.

WHIPLASH

The whiplash injury is a much litigated one and the source of great mirth from a sceptical public. However, to the sufferer it can involve anything from a mild pain in the neck to a very severe low back pain. It usually arises as a result of one car running into the rear of another in which the driver and his/her passengers sustain injury. The pain can be immediate or it can take a period of time to manifest itself. The injured party may experience difficulty (great or otherwise) doing things that one takes for granted, e.g. fastening one's shoelaces, hanging washing on the clothes-line, cleaning windows and bending or lifting.

The Statute of Limitations 1957 lays down limitation periods in which the intended plaintiff (victim) must bring his action against the defendant. No one should be placed in the intolerable position of not knowing when he/she may be sued. Generally speaking, in personal injuries, the injured party of mature years (eighteen years and over) has three years from the date of the accident. Minors and others have a longer time in which to take their action. The action may be taken in the District Court, the Circuit Court or in the High Court. The appropriate court will be the decision of the intended plaintiff's legal advisers and the decision will be based, by and large, on the medical report(s). If the injured party has recovered quickly and has resumed normal activity, and his medical advisers are reasonably satisfied that no long-term repercussions will arise, then the action may be taken in either the District Court (£5,000 jurisdiction) or in the Circuit Court (£30,000 jurisdiction). The High Court has unlimited jurisdiction in personal injuries. In other words, it is open to the High Court to award whatever sum it deems appropriate to satisfy the plaintiff's claim. At one stage, High Court personal injury cases were heard by a judge and jury. Some time ago, due to the urgings of the insurance companies, an Act of the Oireachtas abolished juries in personal injuries. Therefore, at all three levels every personal injury case is heard by a judge sitting alone.

It is not necessary here to go into all the preparatory work that needs to be completed before a case is ready for hearing. Suffice it to say that, as soon as the pleadings (paperwork) have closed, the action can be set down for trial. In due course, a date will be given and the parties will turn up in court.

The court must address two issues before the matter can be finalised. The two matters are Liability and Quantum. Just because a person sustains injury does not necessarily mean that that person will successfully recover an award for damages. The plaintiff (victim) must allege and prove that someone was negligent and to blame for the injuries he sustained. Liability is, therefore, deciding who is responsible for the accident. In the example given in the opening paragraph above, the passenger, whether in the front or the rear of the car which was hit in the back, cannot be held responsible for the accident and the subsequent injuries sustained. Therefore, that person will recover 100 per cent, whether entirely from the driver of the car behind or partly from his own driver and the second driver. The court may take the view on the evidence presented that there is contributory negligence on the part of the first driver and may find him/her responsible or liable on a percentage basis. If the court finds the first driver responsible 25 per cent, then the second car will be held to be 75 per cent to blame and the injured party will recover 100 per cent.

Having overcome the question of Liability, the next question is Quantum, or value, and this will depend on a number of factors, especially the medical reports. The successful litigant will recover damages which may be *general damages*, for pain and suffering, from the date of the accident to the hearing and from the date of the hearing into the future. In addition, the successful litigant may recover *special damages*, that is, out of pocket expenses and costs as a result of the accident and, finally, legal costs. Not necessarily all costs will be paid, but a portion will be made in the plaintiff's favour.

Not all litigation ends in a hearing in court. The defendant may decide to settle the action out of court to save costs. An assessment is made of the plaintiff's case and if it is abundantly clear that liability is not an issue, the defendant will seek to settle the matter. In such circumstances, the only question to be decided is the question of Quantum or value. Again, the value will be based, by and large, on the medical reports. A word of caution to the reader: once the matter is settled, that is the end of it and it cannot be reopened. Therefore, it is vitally important that the plaintiff be very carefully advised and apprised of the implications of settling his or her case. Many litigants have been less than happy with the final outcome and this may be due to their not asking sufficient questions concerning the implications of the intended settlement.

Before a settlement is finalised, the plaintiff should be satisfied as to his/her long-term medical condition. No medical person can give an absolutely certain prognosis, but a reasonably accurate assessment can be made by assessing all the relevant circumstances (age, work, pre-accident activity, post-accident activity, e.g. sport). If the plaintiff is not happy with the proposed settlement, he/she should instruct his/her solicitors to reject it and to proceed to a hearing. Settlements often collapse because the defendant is not prepared to offer a sum the plaintiff feels his injuries are worth.

Certain consequences may flow from rejecting the settlement. For example, the defendant may decide to make a lodgment. The defendant will lodge in court a sum of money the defendant thinks is sufficient and adequate to satisfy the plaintiff's claim. The question of the lodgment and its implications should be clearly understood by the plaintiff. Let's say that the settlement talks collapse on 1 January and within a week the defendant or his solicitor indicates to the plaintiff that a lodgment has been made. If, at the hearing of the action, the plaintiff fails to be awarded a sum greater than the lodgment, in other words, 'beating the lodgment', the plaintiff will pay both sides' costs from the date of the lodgment. The implications of understanding the lodgment cannot be overstressed. One penny less than the lodgment can be disastrous for the litigant. (The judge hearing the action is not aware of the amount of the lodgment.) If the matter goes to court and if there is no lodgment and the plaintiff or, indeed, the defendant is dissatisfied with the outcome, an appeal may be taken to the court above. Up to High Court level, it will be a complete rehearing of the case but in the Supreme Court it will be in the transcript, i.e. a complete account of the evidence in the court. No oral evidence from either the plaintiff or defendant is heard in the Supreme Court but legal argument on both sides will be heard. The appeal may be on the question of Liability or Quantum or both. It is open to the judge hearing the appeal to:

(i)   let the judgment of the lower court stand;

(ii)   reverse it in its entirety;

(iii) increase or decrease the amount awarded; or

(iv) in the case of a Supreme Court appeal, order a new trial in the High Court.

Index